Multicultural Issues
in School Psychology

Multicultural Issues in School Psychology has been co-published simultaneously as *Journal of Applied School Psychology*, Volume 22, Number 2 2006.

of a variety of group interventions designed to promote students' success in school and life."
(Social Work with Groups Newsletter)

Promoting Success with At-Risk Students: Emerging Perspectives and Practical Approaches, *edited by Louis J. Kruger, PsyD (Vol. 5, No. 3/4, 1990). "Essential to professionals interested in new developments in the education of at-risk students, guidelines for implementation of approaches, and the prevention of student crises and discipline problems." (Virginia Child Protection Newsletter)*

Leadership and Supervision in Special Services: Promising Ideas and Practices, *edited by Leonard C. Burrello, EdD, and David E. Greenburg, EdD (Vol. 4, No. 1/2, 1988). A rich source of ideas for administrative personnel involved in the delivery of special educational programs and services to children with handicapping conditions.*

School-Based Affective and Social Interventions, *edited by Susan G. Forman, PhD (Vol. 3, No. 3/4, 1988). "Provides a valuable starting point for the psychologist, counselor, or other special service provider, special educator, regular classroom teacher, nurse, vice-principal, or other administrator who is willing to get involved in the struggle to help children and adolescents feel good about themselves and get along better in this world." (Journal of Pediatric Nursing)*

Facilitating Cognitive Development: International Perspectives, Programs, and Practices, *edited by Milton S. Schwebel and Charles A. Maher, PsyD (Vol. 3, No. 1/2, 1986). Experts discuss the vital aspects of programs and services that will facilitate cognitive development in children and adolescents.*

Emerging Perspectives on Assessment of Exceptional Children, *edited by Randy Elliot Bennett, EdD, and Charles A. Maher, PsyD (Vol. 2, No. 2/3, 1986). "Contains a number of innovative and promising approaches to the topic of assessment. It is an important addition to the rapidly changing field of special education and should be read by any individual who is interested in the assessment of exceptional children." (Journal of Psychological Assessment)*

Health Promotion in the Schools: Innovative Approaches to Facilitating Physical and Emotional Well-Being, *edited by Joseph E. Zins, Donald I. Wagner, and Charles A. Maher, PsyD (Vol. 1, No. 3, 1985). "Examines new approaches to promoting physical and emotional well-being in the schools. . . . A good introduction to new-style health education." (Curriculum Review)*

Microcomputers and Exceptional Children, *edited by Randy Elliot Bennett, EdD, and Charles A. Maher, PsyD (Vol. 1, No. 1, 1984). "This volume provides both the experienced and novice micro buff with a solid overview of the potential and real uses of the technology with exceptional students." (Alex Thomas, PhD, Port Clinton, Ohio)*

Multicultural Issues in School Psychology

Bonnie K. Nastasi, PhD
Editor

Multicultural Issues in School Psychology has been co-published simultaneously as *Journal of Applied School Psychology*, Volume 22, Number 2 2006.

The Haworth Press, Inc.

New York • London • Victoria (AU)
www.HaworthPress.com

Multicultural Issues in School Psychology has been co-published simultaneously as *Journal of Applied School Psychology*™, Volume 22, Number 2 2006.

The development, preparation, and publication of this work has been undertaken with great care. However, the publisher, employees, editors, and agents of The Haworth Press and all imprints of The Haworth Press, Inc., including The Haworth Medical Press® and Pharmaceutical Products Press®, are not responsible for any errors contained herein or for consequences that may ensue from use of materials or information contained in this work. With regard to case studies, identities and circumstances of individuals discussed herein have been changed to protect confidentiality. Any resemblance to actual persons, living or dead, is entirely coincidental.

The Haworth Press is committed to the dissemination of ideas and information according to the highest standards of intellectual freedom and the free exchange of ideas. Statements made and opinions expressed in this publication do not necessarily reflect the views of the Publisher, Directors, management, or staff of The Haworth Press, Inc., or an endorsement by them.

Cover design by Kerry Mack

Library of Congress Cataloging-in-Publication Data

Multicultural issues in school psychology / Bonnie K. Nastasi, editor.
    p. cm.
    "Multicultural issues in school psychology has been co-published simultaneously as Journal of Applied School Psychology, Volume 22, Number 2, 2006."
    Includes bibliographical references and index.
    ISBN-13: 978-0-7890-3464-9 (hard cover : alk. paper)
    ISBN-10: 0-7890-3464-6 (hard cover : alk. paper)
    ISBN-13: 978-0-7890-3465-6 (soft cover : alk. paper)
    ISBN-10: 0-7890-3465-4 (soft cover : alk. paper)
  1. School psychology–Cross-cultural studies. 2. Multiculturalism. I. Nastasi, Bonnie K.
    LB1027.55.M85 2006
    371.4–dc22
                                          2006028631

Indexing, Abstracting & Website/Internet Coverage

This section provides you with a list of major indexing & abstracting services and other tools for bibliographic access. That is to say, each service began covering this periodical during the year noted in the right column. Most Websites which are listed below have indicated that they will either post, disseminate, compile, archive, cite or alert their own Website users with research-based content from this work. (This list is as current as the copyright date of this publication.)

(continued)

* **Exact start date to come**

(continued)

*Special Bibliographic Notes related to special journal issues
(separates) and indexing/abstracting:*

- indexing/abstracting services in this list will also cover material in any "separate" that is co-published simultaneously with Haworth's special thematic journal issue or DocuSerial. Indexing/abstracting usually covers material at the article/chapter level.
- monographic co-editions are intended for either non-subscribers or libraries which intend to purchase a second copy for their circulating collections.
- monographic co-editions are reported to all jobbers/wholesalers/approval plans. The source journal is listed as the "series" to assist the prevention of duplicate purchasing in the same manner utilized for books-in-series.
- to facilitate user/access services all indexing/abstracting services are encouraged to utilize the co-indexing entry note indicated at the bottom of the first page of each article/chapter/contribution.
- this is intended to assist a library user of any reference tool (whether print, electronic, online, or CD-ROM) to locate the monographic version if the library has purchased this version but not a subscription to the source journal.
- individual articles/chapters in any Haworth publication are also available through the Haworth Document Delivery Service (HDDS).

Multicultural Issues in School Psychology

CONTENTS

ABOUT THE EDITOR

Bonnie K. Nastasi, PhD, is Director of the School Psychology specialization and full-time faculty member in the School of Psychology at Walden University. She received her doctorate in School Psychology in 1986 from Kent State University. She has taught graduate courses in psychology for 14 years at Illinois State University, University of Connecticut, University at Albany, NY, and Walden. Before joining Walden full-time,she served as Associate Director of Interventions at the Institute for Community Research, Hartford, CT, for 6 years. Her areas of specialization are school- and community mental health promotion and health risk prevention (drugs and sexual risk); mixed-method (qualitative-quantitative) research; and promoting school psychology internationally. She has worked in the South Asian countries of Sri Lanka and India since 1995 on research and development projects focused on mental health promotion and health risk prevention. Dr. Nastasi is currently engaged in long-term recovery efforts to foster student adjustment and coping following natural disasters in Sri Lanka and New Orleans. Dr. Nastasi is primary author of three books: *School-based Mental Health Services: Creating Comprehensive and Culturally Specific Programs* (APA, 2004); *School Interventions for Children of Alcoholics* (Guilford Press, 1994); and three editions of *Exemplary Mental Health Programs: School Psychologists as Mental Health Service Providers* (NASP, 1997, 1998, 2002). She has published numerous chapters and articles in referred journals; has presented at national and international conferences in psychology, education, and anthropology; and served as Associate Editor for the *School Psychology Review* and *School Psychology Quarterly*. She is former Treasurer of the Society for Study of School Psychology and current Treasurer of Division 16 of American Psychological Association.

About the Contributors

Marty Avant is an Educational Diagnostician in the Leander Independent School District in Leander, TX.

Gary Burkholder is Assistant Dean for Student Success for the College of Social Behavioral Sciences at Walden University.

Brian J. Dew is Assistant Professor of Counseling and Counselor Education at Georgia State University, and Research Faculty for the Center for Research on School Safety, School Climate and Classroom Management. He is the President of the American Counseling Association's Division for Gay, Lesbian, and Bisexual Issues in Counseling (AGLBIC).

Emily C. Graybill is a doctoral student in the School Psychology Program at Georgia State University.

Chryse Hatzichristou is Professor of School Psychology and Director of the Center for Research and Practice of School Psychology, Department of Psychology, University of Athens, Greece.

Christopher C. Henrich is Assistant Professor of Psychology at Georgia State University, and Research Faculty for the Center for Research on School Safety, School Climate and Classroom Management.

John H. Hitchcock is Senior Associate with Caliber, and ICF International Company.

Colette L. Ingraham is Professor in the School Psychology Program at San Diego State University.

Asoka Jayasena is Retired Professor of Education at University of Peradeniya, Sri Lanka.

Jason P. Kaplan is a doctoral student in the School and Counseling Psychology Doctoral Program, Counseling and Applied Educational Psychology Department, at Northeastern University.

Aikaterini Lampropoulou is school psychologist and PhD Candidate in School Psychology, Department of Psychology, University of Athens, Greece.

Chieh Li is Associate Professor and Director of the School Psychology Program at Northeastern University.

Emilia C. Lopez is the Director of the Bilingual and Multicultural Specializations at Queens College, City University of New York. She is also the editor of the *Journal of Educational and Psychological Consultation.*

Konstantina Lykitsakou is school psychologist and PhD Candidate in School Psychology, Department of Psychology, University of Athens, Greece.

Megan L. Marshall is a doctoral student in the School Psychology Program at Georgia State University.

Joel Meyers is Professor of School Psychology at Georgia State University, and the Director of the Center for Research on School Safety, School Climate and Classroom Management.

Bonnie K. Nastasi is Director of the School Psychology Program at Walden University.

Evelyn R. Oka is Associate Professor and Co-Director of the School Psychology Program at Michigan State University.

Samuel O. Ortiz is Associate Professor in the Department of Psychology at St. John's University, New York.

Sreeroopa Sarkar is Director of Masters Degree Programs in Psychology and Faculty Member at Walden University.

Rebecca B. Skoczylas is a graduate student in the School Psychology Program at Georgia State University.

Kris Varjas is Assistant Professor of School Psychology at Georgia State University, and Research Faculty for the Center for Research on School Safety, School Climate and Classroom Management.

Ena Vazquez-Nuttall is Professor in the School Psychology Program at Northeastern University.

Zachary Williamson was a graduate student in the School Psychology Program at Georgia State University. He currently is working as a School Psychologist for Rutland Psychoeducational Services in Athens, GA.

Multicultural Issues
in School Psychology Practice:
Introduction

Bonnie K. Nastasi

Walden University

SUMMARY. This special volume provides theoretical and empirical models for multicultural school psychology practice, based on the work of the contributing authors who are engaged in efforts to address multicultural or cross-cultural issues in practice and/or to provide culturally specific or culturally embedded services in schools. This introductory article describes the foundations of a participatory culture-specific model for school psychology practice: ecological-developmental theory, ethnographic and participatory action research, and participatory consultation (PCSM; Nastasi et al., 2004). These foundations provide a framework for the remaining articles in this collection, which address multicultural issues related to assessment, intervention, consultation, systems/community intervention, home-school partnerships and adoption of evidence-based interventions. The article concludes with a discussion of the school psychologist's role in multicultural practice and implications for development of culturally competent school psychologists. doi:10.1300/J370v22n02_01 *[Article copies available for a fee from The Haworth Document Delivery Service: 1-800-HAWORTH. E-mail address: <docdelivery@haworthpress.com> Website: <http://www.HaworthPress.com> © 2006 by The Haworth Press, Inc. All rights reserved.]*

[Haworth co-indexing entry note]: "Multicultural Issues in School Psychology Practice: Introduction." Nastasi, Bonnie K. Co-published simultaneously in *Journal of Applied School Psychology* (The Haworth Press, Inc.) Vol. 22, No. 2, 2006, pp. 1-11; and: *Multicultural Issues in School Psychology* (ed: Bonnie K. Nastasi) The Haworth Press, Inc., 2006, pp. 1-11. Single or multiple copies of this article are available for a fee from The Haworth Document Delivery Service [1-800-HAWORTH, 9:00 a.m. - 5:00 p.m. (EST). E-mail address: docdelivery@haworthpress.com].

KEYWORDS. Culture, ethnicity, language, schools, school psychologists

With increasing awareness of the global community and the needs of the culturally diverse population within the United States, school psychologists have become cognizant of the limitations of ethnocentric perspectives and practices. Cultural considerations potentially affect all areas of school psychology practice, including assessment, intervention, consultation, systems change, and home-school-community partnerships. Despite the need for addressing culture in practice, the school psychology literature provides minimal guidance or exemplars for engaging in such practice. The purpose of this special issue is to provide theoretical and empirical models for practice, based on the work of the contributing authors, all of whom are engaged in efforts to develop culturally specific or culturally embedded school psychology practices or to address multicultural or cross-cultural issues in practice. Although much of this work is in its early stages, it can provide guidance in theory development, research, training, policy, and practice relevant to school psychology. Several themes emerge from the work represented in this volume: (a) importance of an ecological perspective; (b) broad and varied definitions of culture; (c) involvement of stakeholders in decision making; (d) innovative approaches to data collection and intervention design; and (e) reconsideration of the school psychologist's role. This introductory article presents a model to guide examination of approaches to addressing multicultural issues in school psychology practice. In addition, the school psychologist's role in multicultural practice and implications for professional development of culturally competent school psychologists are discussed.

PARTICIPATORY CULTURE-SPECIFIC MODELS

To facilitate the development of culturally specific approaches to school psychology practice, Nastasi and colleagues have proposed Participatory Culture-Specific Models (PCSM) for intervention (PCSIM; Nastasi, Moore, & Varjas, 2004; Nastasi, Varjas, Sarkar, & Jayasena, 1998; Nastasi, Varjas, Schensul, Silva, Schensul, & Ratnayake, 2000) and consultation (PCSC; Nastasi, Varjas, Bernstein, & Jayasena, 2000). The models draw on contemporary approaches to school psychology (e.g., consultation, systems change), but extend those approaches through integration of thinking and methods from other disciplines (e.g., anthropology, public health; see Nastasi et al., 2000). The conceptual, methodological and procedural foundations of PCSM include *ecological-developmental theory* (conceptual foundation; Bronfenbrenner, 1989), *ethnography* and *participatory action research* (methodological foundations) and *participatory consultation* (procedural foundation). Each of these foundations is briefly described below and illustrated in the papers contained in this publication. In addition, the concept of cultural specificity in PCSM is defined, and alternative concepts proposed by contributing authors are discussed. (A detailed discussion and illustration of the PCSIM can be found in Nastasi et al., 2004.)

Ecological-Developmental Theory

Underlying much of the current work in school psychology is an ecological-developmental perspective stemming from Bronfenbrenner's (1989) theory. The ecology of the child is conceptualized as a series of concentric circles in which the individual (child, student) is embedded within his/her immediate social-cultural context (microsystem; e.g., family, school, peer group), which is embedded within a larger social-cultural context (exosystem; e.g., school, extended family, extended peer network), which in turn is embedded in a larger social-cultural-historical context (macrosystem; e.g., community, society, country). A key assumption of the model is that the individual is influenced directly by the microsystem and indirectly by the surrounding contexts (exosystem, macrosystem) and by the interaction of those contexts (mesosystem; e.g., school-family relationships). In addition, the influences are reciprocal such that the individual also influences the ecological system (e.g., through student-teacher, parent-child, or peer-peer interactions). Furthermore, the mutual accommodation of the individual and context evolves over the life span so that prior experiences influence later functioning and interactions in similar and novel situations (e.g., early school experiences influence later school experiences).

Addressing multicultural issues in school psychology practice requires particular attention to the cultural aspects of both the individual's experiences and the ecological systems. Culture is typically reflected in the values, beliefs, language, practices, and behavioral norms of the members of the culture; and extends far beyond demographic categories such as race, ethnicity or gender (Nastasi et al., 2004). With increasing complexity of the child's ecology (e.g., across family, school, peer group) and the potential diversity among children and adults within a classroom or school, the cultural considerations expand exponentially. Thus, giving due consideration to culture can be a daunting task for any school psychologist. The articles in this collection provide examples of the manner in which ecological considerations can influence school psychology practice and the range of approaches for addressing cultural issues from an ecological perspective. Hitchcock, Sarkar, Nastasi, Burkholder, Varjas, and Jayasena (this volume) and Hatzichristou, Lampropoulou, and Lykitsakou (this volume) address ecological considerations at societal level in the development of assessment tools and school psychological services, respectively. Varjas et al. (this volume) address ecological considerations related to peer victimization with particular attention to peer and school contexts. Lopez's work (this volume) focuses on the ecology of the instructional environment for English Language Learners (ELLs). Vasquez-Nuttall, Li, and Kaplan (this volume) propose an ecological model for promoting home-school partnerships, requiring a specific focus on mesosystem variables (i.e., those related to interaction of home and school ecologies). In their discussion of cultural considerations relevant to evidence-based practice, Ingraham and Oka (this volume) endorse a strong contextual perspective which requires detailed examination and documentation of ecological factors in the conduct of research and application of evidence-based interventions (EBIs).

Ethnography and Participatory Action Research

Essential to multicultural practice is the systematic examination of culture as manifested in the relevant ecological systems, including the culture of the individual (e.g., student, parent, teacher, psychologist), the targeted context (e.g., classroom, family), the larger social contexts (e.g., school, community), and the potential cultural conflicts across ecosystems (e.g., clash of home-school or adult-adolescent cultures). Furthermore, development of culturally appropriate/specific, multicultural or cross-cultural practices requires a data-based problem-solving approach consistent with reflective practice (Nastasi et al., 2004). The integration of systematic examination of culture and data-based problem solving is reflected in the combined use of ethnographic and participatory action research within PCSM. Ethnography and participatory action research are briefly described in this section.[1]

Ethnography. Ethnography (the study of culture and a form of qualitative research) is particularly well suited to systematic study leading to multicultural school psychology practice. Within PCSM, ethnography plays a key role in conducting formative and evaluative research to ensure that cultural factors are well understood and well represented in practice (Nastasi et al., 2004). Hitchcock et al. (this volume) used ethnographic methods (e.g., in-depth individual and group interviews), to examine key constructs related to definitions and promotion of mental health within the Sri Lankan culture, as an initial step to development of culture-specific assessment tools. Varjas et al. (this volume) used ethnographic methods (participant observation, key informant interviews, in-depth interviews) in formative research to identify cultural factors relevant to peer victimization within a school context and in evaluation research during a pilot peer victimization intervention program. Ethnographic methods can be applied within a case study approach, such as that illustrated in Vasquez-Nuttall et al. (this volume) to examine cultural factors relevant to work with culturally diverse families. Furthermore, developing and evaluating contextualized interventions requires the use of qualitative research (e.g., ethnographic) methods that can facilitate detailed examination of learning contexts for the purposes of problem identification (Lopez, this volume) or detailed documentation relevant to examining treatment integrity and facilitating transferability (Ingraham & Oka, this volume). Finally, ethnographic methods can be applied to comprehensive change efforts at a school system or community level such as those described by Hatzichristou et al. (this volume).

Participatory Action Research (PAR). PAR, with roots in applied anthropology (Greenwood, Whyte, & Harkavy, 1993; Nastasi, 1998; Schensul, 1998; Schensul & Schensul, 1992), is consistent with collaborative data-based problem solving approaches in school psychology. PAR involves a recursive theory-research-action process in which theory and research drive the development of interventions (practice or action) directed at social change. The evaluation (through research) of these efforts subsequently informs adaptation of theory and models of intervention. PAR is distinguished from action research (AR) by the involvement of stakeholders (individuals or organizations with vested interests or resources) in all phases of theory-research-action process. For the individual engaged in psychological practice, PAR involving key stakeholders could facilitate the adaptation EBIs to meet the needs of particular cultural groups or contexts (see Ingraham & Oka, this volume). PAR is explicitly or implicitly reflected in all the work presented in this volume.

Participatory (Collaborative) Consultation

Another critical foundation of PCSM is participatory (or collaborative) consultation, which is germane to the practice of school psychology and consistent with PAR. Within PCSM, participatory consultation refers to the process of co-constructing interventions or change efforts in partnership with key stakeholders (Nastasi et al., 2000). The term *participatory* (vs. collaboration) denotes equal involvement of stakeholders in the process of design, implementation and evaluation of interventions; the goal of which is promoting ownership, sustainability and institutionalization as well as culture specificity (Nastasi et al., 2004). The approaches described in this volume all involve some level of participation by key stakeholders in the process of understanding cultural factors and/or developing culturally appropriate interventions.

Cultural Specificity

The primary goal of PCSM is achieving *cultural specificity*. Within this model, cultural specificity is defined as follows:

> Cultural specificity implies that critical elements of the intervention (e.g., intervention strategies and targeted competencies) are relevant to the targeted culture, make use of the language of the population, and reflect the values and beliefs of members of the culture. Inherent in this model is the assumption that one cannot separate person from culture and that understanding the culture is essential to understanding the individual. In addition, change efforts cannot be solely person-centered, but must address the role of culture in promoting and sustaining behavior patterns. (Nastasi, 1998, p. 169)

As noted in the final article by Ortiz (this volume), several terms are proposed for discussing issues relevant to multiculturalism. Varjas et al. (this volume) adopt the term *culture specificity* in their application of the PCSIM. The work of Hitchcock et al. (this volume) is considered by the authors to reflect a *cross-cultural* perspective. Vasquez et al. (this volume) adopt the term *culturally diverse* in discussing issues related to home-school partnerships that involve immigrant, bilingual, or ethnic minority families. Hatzichristou et al. (this volume) differentiate between the terms *multicultural, cross-cultural* and *intercultural*; and proposes the use of the term *metacultural* to depict "multicultural systems as integrating the various elements of its consisting cultural groups into new dynamic outcomes" (p. 110). Ingraham and Oka (this volume) distinguish between culturally specific and *culturally embedded*, using the latter term to depict the contextualized (embedded) nature of interventions. Similarly, Lopez (this volume) emphasizes the embedded nature of instruction for English Language Learners (ELLs) and the importance of considering the learner, the task and the intervention when providing instructional consultation with teachers of ELLs. Readers are encouraged to carefully consider the alternative concepts and distinctions proposed by the contributing authors. The attention to differences in terminology related to multicultural issues speaks to the complexity of the topic.

SCHOOL PSYCHOLOGIST'S ROLE: IMPLICATIONS FOR PROFESSIONAL DEVELOPMENT

Moving beyond ethnocentric perspectives and practices requires development of multicultural competence and careful consideration of the role, functions and identity of school psychologists. Multicultural competence requires lifetime professional commitment to developing awareness, knowledge, and skills relevant to understanding one's own cultural experiences and worldview and those of the client and relevant stakeholders, and integrating that information into culturally appropriate contextualized practice (Ivey & Ivey, 2003; Nastasi et al., 2004). Achieving competence necessitates adopting a reflective approach to practice that is consistent with action research and scientist-practitioner models, and embodies what Pintner and Sakamoto (2005) refer to as *critical consciousness*. Pinter and Sakamoto's conception involves consideration of both personal and structural level factors that influence action. Among the key considerations on a personal level are the psychologist's individual/professional identity and social position (e.g., privileged vs. oppressed) in relation to that of the client. At a structural level, they emphasize the importance of an egalitarian and ethnographic approach, consistent with the participatory and methodological features of PCSM (described above). Pinter and Sakamoto caution psychologists of the potential limitations of critical consciousness, which may lead to reinforcing stereotypes and/or over-reliance on "cookbook" approaches to multicultural practice (e.g., prescribed approaches for working with particular ethnic groups in the U.S.).

The practice models described and proposed by the contributors to this special issue entail specific competencies. For example, the work reflected in Hitchcock et al. (this volume) and Varjas et al. (this volume) necessitates competence in mixed (qualitative-quantitative) methods research leading to culturally specific instrument and intervention development. Ensuring culturally embedded evidence-based practice, as described by Ingraham and Oka (this volume), requires that school psychologists possess competence in developing, adapting and contextualizing EBIs, including competence in mixed-methods research. Lopez (this volume) expands models of instructional consultation to incorporate considerations relevant to English Language Learners, such as knowledge of second language acquisition. Similarly, Vasquez-Nuttal et al.'s (this volume) extension of home-school collaboration/involvement models requires skills relevant to understanding the culture and experiences of families from culturally diverse backgrounds. In addition, their use of case study approach has implications for developing competence in qualitative and mixed-methods single case study designs. Finally, the systems/community model illustrated by Hatzichristou et al. (this volume) demands multicultural competence in systems change and capacity building, comprehensive service delivery, program development and evaluation, and professional training of school psychologists and other school professionals.

The work reflected in this publication points to the need to expand the role and identity of school psychologists to include competencies relevant to multicultural practice. The work of several of the authors involves the use of qualitative and mixed-methods, indicating a need to expand current research and evaluation competencies of school psychologists. Much of the work reflects an expansion of current competencies in assessment, intervention, consultation and systems change to include approaches that ensure culturally and contextually relevant service delivery. Ingraham and Oka (this volume) outline specific considerations for school psychologists interested in adopting or transporting EBIs to new populations and contexts. The latest revision of the *Procedural and Coding Manual for Review of EBIs*, developed by the Task Force on Evidence Based Interventions in School Psychology,[2] includes criteria pertaining to evaluating the extent to which EBIs address cultural considerations. In addition, the work of Hatzichristou et al. (this volume) emphasizes the importance of competencies related to comprehensive service delivery and community capacity building.

Finally, developing multicultural competence is best viewed as a life-long process of professional development that involves critical consciousness (see Pinter & Sakamoto, 2005) as part of reflective practice. Such a process is necessary to ensure that school psychologists give continual attention to their own cultural experiences and worldviews, assume a position of openness to learning about culture from clients and stakeholders, and develop skills necessary for engaging in culturally specific and culturally embedded practice. In addition, engaging in critical consciousness and multicultural practice must be balanced with consideration of potential barriers related to stereotyping or reliance on prescribed approaches for specific cultural groups. Only with deliberate attention to culture and context in school psychology practice can we be prepared to meet the needs of a culturally diverse national and global community.

NOTES

1. A full articulation of ethnography, qualitative and participatory action research is beyond the scope of the article. Readers are encouraged to consult the following sources: Bernard (1995); Camic, Rhodes, and Yardley (2003); Creswell (1997); Denzin and Lincoln (2000); Fetterman (1998); LeCompte, Millroy, and Preissle (1992); Lincoln and Guba (1985); Miles and Huberman (1994); Moustakas (1994); Ryan and Bernard (2000); Schensul and LeCompte (1999); Spradley (1979, 1980); Stake (1995); Strauss and Corbin (1990); Wolcott (1994).

2. For the most recent version of the manual, contact Thomas R. Kratochwill, PhD, School Psychology Program, University of Wisconsin, Madison. Relevant publications include: Kratochwill and Stoiber, 2002a, 2002b; Nastasi and Schensul, 2005.

REFERENCES

Bernard, H. R. (1995). *Research methods in anthropology: Qualitative and quantitative approaches.* Thousand Oaks, CA: Sage.

Bronfenbrenner, U. (1989). Ecological systems theory. In R. Vasta (Ed.), *Annals of Child Development* (Vol. 6, pp. 187-249). Greenwich, CT: JAI Press.

Camic, P. M, Rhodes, J. E., & Yardley, L. (Ed.). (2003). *Qualitative research in psychology: Expanding perspectives in methodology and design.* Washington, DC: APA.

Creswell, J. W. (1997). *Qualitative inquiry and research design.* Thousand Oaks, CA: Sage.

Denzin, N. K., & Lincoln, Y. S. (Eds.). (2000). *Handbook of qualitative research* (2nd ed.). Thousand Oaks, CA: Sage.

Fetterman, D. (1998, 2nd ed). *Ethnography: Step by step.* Thousand Oaks, CA: Sage.

Greenwood, D. J., Whyte, W. F., & Harkavy, I. (1993). Participatory action research as a process and as a goal. *Human Relations, 46,* 175-192.

Hatzichristou, C., Lampropoulou, A., & Lykitsakou, K. (2006). Addressing cultural factors in development of system interventions. *Journal of Applied School Psychology, 22,* 103-126.

Hitchcock, J.H., Sarkar, S., Nastasi, B.K., Burkholder, G., Varjas, K., & Jayasena, A. (2006). Validating culture- and gender-specific constructs: A mixed-method approach to advance assessment procedures in cross-cultural settings. *Journal of Applied School Psychology, 22,* 13-33.

Ingraham, C.L., & Oka, E. R. (2006). Multicultural issues in evidence-based interventions. *Journal of Applied School Psychology, 22,* 127-149.

Ivey, A. E., & Ivey, M. B. (2003). *Intentional interviewing and counseling: Facilitating client development in a multicultural society* (5th ed.). Pacific Grove, CA: Brooks/Cole.

Kratochwill, T. R., & Stoiber, K. C. (2002a). Evidence-based interventions in school psychology: Conceptual foundations of the *Procedural and Coding Manual* of Division 16 and the Society for the Study of School Psychology Task Force. *School Psychology Quarterly, 17,* 341-389.

Kratochwill, T. R., & Stoiber, K. C. (2002b). *Procedural and coding manual for review of evidence-based interventions.* University of Wisconsin-Madison.

LeCompte, M. D., Millroy, W. L., & Preissle, J. (Eds.). (1992). *The handbook of qualitative research in education.* San Diego, CA: Academic Press.

Lincoln, Y. S., & Guba, E. G. (1985). *Naturalistic inquiry.* Thousand Oaks, CA: Sage.

Lopez, E. C. (2006). Targeting English Language Learners, tasks, and treatments in instructional consultation. *Journal of Applied School Psychology, 22,* 59-79.

Miles, M. B., & Huberman, A. M. (1994). *Qualitative data analysis* (2nd ed.). Thousand Oaks, CA: Sage.

Moustakas, C. (1994). *Phenomenological research methods.* Thousand Oaks, CA: Sage.

Nastasi, B. K. (1998). A model for mental health programming in schools and communities. *School Psychology Review, 27,* 165-174.

Nastasi, B. K., Moore, R. B., & Varjas, K. M. (2004). *School-based mental health services: Creating comprehensive and culturally specific programs.* Washington, DC: American Psychological Association.

Nastasi, B. K., & Schensul, S. L. (2005). Contributions of qualitative research to the validity of intervention research. Special issue of *Journal of School Psychology, 43* (3), 177-195.

Nastasi, B. K., Varjas, K., Bernstein, R., & Jayasena, A. (2000). Conducting participatory culture-specific consultation: A global perspective on multicultural consultation. *School Psychology Review, 29,* 401-413.

Nastasi, B. K., Varjas, K., Sarkar, S., & Jayasena, A. (1998). Participatory model of mental health programming: Lessons learned from work in a developing country. *School Psychology Review, 27,* 260-276.

Nastasi, B. K., Varjas, K., Schensul, S. L., Silva, K. T., Schensul, J. J., Ratnayake, P. (2000). The Participatory Intervention Model: A framework for conceptualizing and promoting intervention acceptability. *School Psychology Quarterly, 15,* 207-232.

Ortiz, S. O. (2006). Multicultural issues in school psychology practice: A critical analysis. *Journal of Applied School Psychology, 22,* 151-167.

Pintner, R. O., & Sakamoto, I. (2005). The role of critical consciousness in multicultural practice: Examining how its strengths become its limitations. *American Journal of Orthopsychiatry, 75,* 684-694.

Schensul, J. J. (1998). Community-based risk prevention with urban youth. *School Psychology Review, 27,* 233-245.

Schensul, J. J., & LeCompte, M. D. (Eds.). (1999). *Ethnographer's toolkit* (Volumes 1 to 7). Walnut Creek, CA: AltaMira Press.

Schensul, J. J., & Schensul, S. L. (1992). Collaborative research: Methods of inquiry for social change. In M. D. LeCompte, W. L. Millroy, & J. Preissle (Eds.). *The handbook of qualitative research in education* (pp. 161-200). San Diego, CA: Academic.

Spradley, J. P. (1979). *The ethnographic interview.* NY: Holt, Rhinehart, Winston.

Spradley, J. P. (1980). *Participant observation.* NY: Holt, Rhinehart, Winston.

Stake, R. (1995). *The art of case study research.* Thousand Oaks, CA: Sage.

Strauss, A., & Corbin, J. (1990). *Basics of qualitative research: Grounded theory procedures and techniques.* Thousand Oaks, CA: Sage.

Varjas, K., Meyers, J., Henrich, C.C., Graybill, E.C., Dew, B.J., Marshall, M.L., Williams, Z., Skoczylas, R.B., & Avant, M. (2006). Using a participatory culture-specific intervention model to develop a peer victimization intervention. *Journal of Applied School Psychology, 22,* 35-57.

Vazquez-Nuttall, E., Li, C., & Kaplan, J.P. (2006). Home-school partnerships with culturally diverse families: Challenges and solutions for school personnel. *Journal of Applied School Psychology, 22,* 81-102.

Wolcott, H. F. (1990). *Writing up qualitative research.* Thousand Oaks, CA: Sage.

doi:10.1300/J370v22n02_01

Validating Culture- and Gender-Specific Constructs: A Mixed-Method Approach to Advance Assessment Procedures in Cross-Cultural Settings

John H. Hitchcock

Caliber, an ICF International Company

Sreeroopa Sarkar
Bonnie K. Nastasi
Gary Burkholder

Walden University

Kris Varjas

Georgia State University

Asoka Jayasena

University of Peradeniya, Sri Lanka

An earlier version of this work was presented in a symposium conducted at the 2005 annual meeting of the American Education Research Association. Funding for the early phases of this work was provided through grants to the third author from the Society for the Study of School Psychology and the University at Albany. The authors acknowledge Bill Disch for his support with statistical analysis.

Address correspondence to: John Hitchcock, Caliber, an ICF International Company, 10530 Rosehaven Street, Suite 400, Fairfax, VA 22030 (E-mail: JHitchcock@icfcaliber.com).

[Haworth co-indexing entry note]: "Validating Culture- and Gender-Specific Constructs: A Mixed-Method Approach to Advance Assessment Procedures in Cross-Cultural Settings." Hitchcock, John H. et al. Co-published simultaneously in *Journal of Applied School Psychology* (The Haworth Press, Inc.) Vol. 22, No. 2, 2006, pp. 13-33; and: *Multicultural Issues in School Psychology* (ed: Bonnie K. Nastasi) The Haworth Press, Inc., 2006, pp. 13-33. Single or multiple copies of this article are available for a fee from The Haworth Document Delivery Service [1-800-HAWORTH, 9:00 a.m. - 5:00 p.m. (EST). E-mail address: docdelivery@haworthpress.com].

Available online at http://japps.haworthpress.com
doi:10.1300/J370v22n02_02

13

SUMMARY. Despite on-going calls for developing cultural competency among mental health practitioners, few assessment instruments
consider cultural variation in psychological constructs. To meet the
challenge of developing measures for minority and international students, it is necessary to account for the influence culture may have on the
latent constructs that form a given instrument. What complicates matters
further is that individual factors (e.g., gender) within a culture necessitate additional refinement of factor structures on which such instruments
are based. The current work endeavors to address these concerns by
demonstrating a mixed-methods approach utilized to assess construct validation within a specific culture; and in turn develop culturally-specific instruments. Qualitative methods were used to inform the development of a
structured self-report by gaining detailed knowledge of the target culture
and creating items grounded in interview and observational data. Factor
analysis techniques and triangulation with qualitative analyses validated
these findings. Previous work (Sarkar, 2003) suggested a number of gender-specific perceptions of mental health constructs within the target
culture and these were investigated using additional mixed-method analyses. This article demonstrates an emerging mixed-method technique for
developing culturally sound assessment tools, offers guidance on how to
incorporate the overall approach in assessment, and provides a basis for
thinking critically about the use of existing instruments when working
with diverse populations. doi:10.1300/J370v22n02_02 *[Article copies
available for a fee from The Haworth Document Delivery Service:
1-800-HAWORTH. E-mail address: <docdelivery@haworthpress.com> Website: <http://www.HaworthPress.com> © 2006 by The Haworth Press, Inc. All
rights reserved.]*

KEYWORDS. Assessment, environment, gender, culture, validation

Researchers, policy makers, professional organizations, and mental
health practitioners have repeatedly called attention to the lack of culturally appropriate instruments for ethnic minorities, and the need to
consider cultural factors in mental health programming (American Psychological Association [APA], 1990, 2003; Hall & Okazaki, 2002;
Tanaka, Ebreo, Linn, & Morera, 1998; United States Department of
Health and Human Services [USDHHS], 1999, 2001). An example easily demonstrates why such calls are made. Egeland, Hostetter and
Eshleman (1983) describe how culture can influence assessment

when describing manic behaviors of Old Order Amish suffering from bipolar disorder. Suppose a client presents some of the heightened psychomotor activities associated with the disorder, but otherwise engages in such behaviors as using pay phones, dresses as a typical American might, is sexually active with more than one partner and uses machinery. Absent knowledge of Amish cultural norms, such behavior might easily be viewed as typical and a critical diagnosis could be missed. In this example, even cursory knowledge of the culture reveals just how suspect these behaviors might be, and such recognition would facilitate proper diagnosis. Unfortunately, however, dealing with cultural factors is almost never this straightforward because cultural variation extends into a myriad number of groups and related effects can be subtle (see Castillo, 1997).

Recognizing the complexities of culture represents a critical component of school psychology practice (Rogers et al., 1999); indeed, an empirical base supports the idea that cultural factors play an important role in influencing mental health (APA 2003; Nastasi, Moore, & Varjas, 2004). One explanation is that mental health constructs can be viewed differently by individuals from varied cultures, and perception is influenced by different agents of socialization (e.g., parents, school, and peers) that shape people's beliefs, motives, attitudes, and behavior via socialization practices and expectations. Other variables such as gender can influence how mental health constructs are formed (Brannon, 2002; Sarkar, 2003).

Clear and well-replicated gender differences in mental illnesses like depression, anxiety or schizophrenia have been reviewed by mental health researchers (Romans, 1998). In addition, researchers have shown that physiological, social, psychological, and environmental factors each predict gender differences in terms of mental health constructs (Anshell, Porter, & Quek, 1998; Bird & Harris, 1990; Block & Robins, 1993; Knox, Funk, Elliott, & Bush, 1998; Ptacek, Smith, & Dodge, 1994). Broader socio-cultural factors also play an important role in influencing mental health of individuals through the process of socialization. For instance, socialization practices within a particular culture influence the process of gender role socialization, and researchers have shown how this socialization process has made women more vulnerable to mental health problems (Das & Kemp, 1997; Das Dasgupta, 1996). Through its various agents of socialization, culture fosters development of gender role attitudes, beliefs/stereotypes, and gender-specific behaviors which contribute to the gender differences in mental health constructs (Sarkar, 2003).

In view of the findings of gender-role socialization, investigating the gender differences in mental health constructs in the context of culture is important in providing appropriate services (Baxter, 1998; USDHHS, 1999; 2001). However, there is a dearth of research exploring the role of culture and particularly gender as a cultural variable influencing mental health of individuals; this is especially true in school psychology (Henning-Stout & Brown-Cheatem, 1999). In culturally diverse settings, it is therefore important to explore if there is variation in the definition of mental health constructs. Because many U.S. public school systems represent multicultural contexts (Rogers et al., 1999), the methods described below have clear applications for practice.

What complicates matters is that most psychological instruments do not adequately address the influence of culture on functioning, especially for ethnic minority groups (APA, 2003; Padilla, 2001; USDHHS, 1999, 2001). Some literature suggests that members of a cultural majority tend to be unaware of cultural influences (Sue, Bingham, Porche-Burke & Vasquez, 1999); not surprisingly, researchers often generate instruments with little regard for these factors (Rogler, 1999). Failure to address cultural differences in assessment may therefore lead to problems with construct validity and subsequent efforts to develop interventions based on such assessment.

The objective of this article is, therefore, to address the shortcomings in typical assessment in multicultural settings by demonstrating a mixed-methods approach (see Tashakkori & Teddlie, 2003) for developing and validating culturally specific instruments. The approach combines the use of ethnographic and factor analytic methods to develop and test psychological instruments for students located in Sri Lanka. Some findings presented here will not have immediate relevance outside of Sri Lanka, although the methods can be readily applied to future studies concerned with mental health assessment.

The overall approach entailed several stages: (a) a two-year ethnography conducted in the target culture for the purpose of understanding self-concept issues of adolescents, (b) developing and administering a series of culture-specific instruments that further assess these issues, and (c) demonstrating a mixed-method approach for identifying and validating psychological constructs that are specific to the target culture. An overview of this process can be found in Hitchcock and colleagues (2005). The primary purpose of the earlier publication was to illustrate the methodology with a specific focus on the substantive area of self-concept (as defined by Harter, 1999) and concerns for adolescents in Sri Lanka. This paper extends the previous work through reanalysis of qualitative data (that have not been previously published) and quantitative analysis of a different dataset. The earlier work focused on students' perceptions of how their parents valued various competencies and behaviors; this article focuses on student perceptions of their competencies, and identifying gender-specific differences of these perceptions.

FOUNDATIONS

The work described herein employed the Ecological-Developmental Model of Mental Health (EDMMH; Nastasi et al., 2005) as the conceptual framework for investigating individual and cultural factors related to mental health. The EDMMH has its foundations in psychology and anthropology (Nastasi & DeZolt, 1994; Nastasi, Varjas, Sarkar, Jayasena, 1998) and has been used to guide the development of culture-specific definitions of key constructs through the integration of cultural factors related to the experiences of participants. An ecological approach to human development involves scientific study of a 'progressive, mutual accommodation' between an individual and the environment, in view of the social, cultural and historical contexts (Bronfenbrenner, 1989; 1999). Reflected in the EDMMH is the conceptualization of individual mental health as an interaction among the personal factors–self-perceptions of culturally valued competencies, personal resources, and personal vulnerability, with the cultural factors–cultural norms, competencies valued within the culture, social-cultural stressors and resources, and socialization agents and practices. The model promotes the idea of developing a sense of normative cultural values and any conflicts in values among groups within a context. This allows for an assessment of deviant behavior given cultural norms and stressors derived from lack of resources and competing group needs, both of which are representative of mental health concerns. EDMHH can help assess what might be culturally deviant, but more importantly, it is a framework that is consistent with well-established conceptions of risk and protective factors related to mental health/illness of individuals and prevalence within communities (e.g., Elias & Branden, 1988), models of stress and coping (e.g., Lazarus & Folkman, 1984) and personal-social competence (Nastasi & DeZolt, 1994). It also is consistent with recent developments in the field of positive psychology (Frydenberg, 2002; Snyder & Lopez, 2002).

QUALITATIVE METHODOLOGY AND CONTEXT

The research involved the combined use of qualitative (e.g., interviews, focus groups) and quantitative (rating scales) data collection methods to assess the contextual environment of adolescents in Sri Lanka. The study was conducted within the municipality of Kandy, the second largest city in the country with a population of approximately 100,000. Its schools draw students from the urban community and surrounding villages and the socioeconomic status of community members ranges from lower to upper class (Nastasi et al., 2004).The qualitative study was formative in nature and involved the assessment of the mental health needs of adolescents (see Nastasi et al., 2004). This study was conducted with the long-term goal of developing school-based mental health programs in that country. The findings from that work were used to develop and evaluate a culture-specific mental health assessment tool and intervention program for promoting mental health among school-age children in Sri Lanka.

Sri Lanka has experienced advances in education, health and general standard of living (United Nations Development Programme, 2002; The World Bank in Sri Lanka, 2003). However, the last twenty years of Sri Lankan history has been marked by internal tension resulting from high unemployment rates, civil war, ethnic tension and the youth insurrection (1985-1991; Gunaratna, 1990). These factors have contributed to an unstable economy with dwindling per capita income as well as political unrest and mental health problems among the youth. In an effort to gather data on the mental health of students, researchers conducted group interviews with adolescents (33 groups) and teachers (18 groups), and individual interviews with principals from 18 schools to explore the following constructs: (a) cultural definition of mental health/personal-social competence and adjustment difficulties, (b) cultural mechanisms for socialization and development of mental health/personal-social competence, (c) social stressors as viewed by the adolescents, (d) mechanisms/personal resources for coping with those and other everyday life stressors, and (e) existing resources within the schools and community for securing mental health services. The interviews focused on gathering a wide range of data with regard to the definition of key constructs. Interviews were therefore conducted in an open-ended, semi-structured format (Nastasi, Varjas, Sarkar & Jayasena, 1998.)

Interview questions were generated in collaboration with an educational sociologist/teacher educator and a child psychiatrist in Sri Lanka who had experience in schools (Nastasi et al., 1998). Additionally, questions were asked regarding more specific mental health related issues (e.g., stressors the youth face with regard to academics, types of academic adjustment difficulties that are prevalent among adolescents, family problems and related adjustment difficulties in the children, and the ways in which children and adolescents cope with family problems). Data were coded to identify and define the culture-specific individual and cultural constructs. Efforts were made to understand the educational and psychological concerns of students through their own perspective, as well as those of school professionals. Specific issues noted were high rates of mental health concerns such as substance abuse among peers and parents, stress associated with dating and teacher/parent interest in limiting interaction between the genders, and suicide. A variety of educational concerns associated with a high stakes examination system and limited school resources also were noted. Finally, the data reflected gender differences in several mental health constructs. For example, girls discussed sexual harassment, lack of freedom compared to their male peers and differential expectations for women; whereas boys expressed concern about violence, corruption, and unemployment. [See Nastasi et al., 1998 for full report of methods and initial results.] In view of these findings, a re-analysis of qualitative data was performed to explore the gender differences in the definition of mental health constructs. These analyses formed the basis for a key approach that can combine quantitative and qualitative findings–ethnographic surveys.

QUANTITATIVE METHODOLOGY

Ethnographically informed instruments are designed to reflect the experiences and constructs relevant to the target population (Schensul & LeCompte, 1999), thus yielding culture-specific measures. From the qualitative data, we developed self-report measures designed to assess adolescents' perceived competencies and perceived value of the competencies from their own perspective and that of parents, teachers, and peers. The instruments used the Likert-scale (3- point; 1 = not at all, 2 = some, 3 = a lot) response format. On the perceived competencies measure (the focus of this paper), adolescents were asked to rate themselves on a set of culturally defined competencies. Scale and item construction were designed to reflect the full variation of data across age, gender, ethnicity, and ecological context. After piloting, back translating (e.g., English → Sinhalese → English, to insure accuracy of meaning) and refining via consultation with local experts with knowledge of the target culture, the instrument was administered in written form to students ($n = 611$; 315 males, 296 females), grades 7-12, ages 12-19, across six schools which represented the range of the student population in terms of ethnicity, religion, and socioeconomic status. For further discussion of instrument development, see Hitchcock and colleagues (2005).

The strategy used for the quantitative analysis included a principal components analysis (PCA) of the items in the survey instrument. Promax (oblique) rotation was used to account for an expected correlation among components. Items loading less than .30 on any scale, as well as complex items (those whose factor loadings across scales differed by less than .20) were removed. Cronbach's alpha, a measure of internal consistency, was computed for all scales for the total sample and by gender. Multivariate analysis of variance (MANOVA) was used to compare first the scale scores resulting from the factor analysis by gender, then the individual items on any scale that demonstrated significant differences between boys and girls.

FINDINGS FROM QUALITATIVE ANALYSES

Formative qualitative data were collected by asking students and teachers to describe characteristics of socially-acceptable and unacceptable behavior patterns for boys and girls. Analysis of these data provided evidence of (1) socially-acceptable "suitable" behavior, (2) socially-unacceptable "unsuitable" behavior and (3) behavior that reflected attention to the personal and interpersonal needs of adolescents (see Table 1). Overall, gender differences in how unsuitable behavior is defined were noted. That is, both males and females recognized a broader unsuitable behavior construct but differed when defining it. In terms of suitable behavior, both genders defined it the same way but differences were noted in the degree of expected compliance, with girls generally reporting that they were expected to engage in socially-acceptable behaviors more so than boys. In the area of personal/interpersonal needs, minor gender differences were reflected in the restricted movement and lack of independence and freedom of girls. Following is an overview of each construct.

Suitable Behavior

In group interviews, both male and female adolescents described suitable behavior to include "good" behavior and obedience (see Table 1). For example, suitable behavior entails following school rules and lis-

TABLE 1. Definition of Suitable and Unsuitable Behavior with Gender Differences Highlighted

Cross-Gender Definitions of Suitable Behavior	
Well behaved, Obedient, Disciplined, Humble, Respect elders, Helpful, Loyal, Trustworthy, Supportive, Guides others (e.g., to correct path), Makes effort for best performance in academics	
Male-Specific Reponses	Female-Specific Responses
Obey laws of the country, Leader, Possesses the ability to address and solve problems, Avoids trouble	Follows rules, Talks and behaves nicely with people, Loves the country–protects it, Performs community services, Sets example for others, Treats and loves everyone equally–irrespective of ethnic origin
Cross-Gender Definitions of Unsuitable Behavior	
Ill behaved (e.g., rude, tease girls), Abusive (e.g., use abusive/foul languages), Disruptive (e.g., interrupt others' work), Noncompliance, School truancy, Neglects responsibilities and/or obligations, Not helpful (e.g., do not help friends in trouble)	
Male-Specific Reponses	Female-Specific Responses
Throws tantrum, Pouts, Runs away from home, Betrays friends, Aggressive (e.g., fights, argues; Abusive), Abuses alcohol, drugs, Steals or robs, Joins the gang, carries weapons	Does not follow etiquette, Lies, Stubborn, Interfering, Disruptive, Mistreats others, Slanders, Does not love the country, Having romantic relationship with boys, Acts like a boy

tening to adults. Both male and female students in Sri Lanka argued that respect for elders is a major attribute of culturally valued suitable behaviors. Suitable behavior also was characterized as conducting oneself well, such as by being well disciplined, humble, loyal, and trustworthy. Respondents from both genders revealed that culturally acceptable suitable behavior also included being performance-oriented (e.g., performs well and assumes leadership in extracurricular and competitive activities).

As previously noted, there were differences between boys and girls in terms of suitable behavior that focused on degree of compliance expectations. That is, females were expected to exhibit more of these behaviors than boys. Female students described a girl showing suitable behavior as one who listens to what parents and teachers say, and observes the rules and regulations. Examples of such behaviors might be trying to avoid troubling others, giving up a seat to a teacher when they are on the bus, and observing customs and tradition of the country. Girls indicated that such an individual talks nicely with others, sets a good example for others, performs community services, and loves the country. Male students also indicated that such a person obeys the law and does not harm others, but focused more on avoiding disruptive behavior, as opposed to following a broad set of expectations.

Unsuitable Behavior

Both males and females referred to unsuitable behavior as being "ill behaved" (e.g., gets drunk and misbehaves with girls), aggressive (e.g., fights with other people), abusive (e.g., uses foul languages), and/or disruptive (e.g., disrupts the classroom). Noncompliance (e.g., refuses to comply with rules; does not obey elders) and school truancy were other attributes of unsuitable behavior among adolescents. Overall, descriptions of unsuitable behavior appeared to be readily identifiable in interview responses. Despite this finding, the qualitative data indicated important gender differences in how the construct is defined. Unsuitable behavior among Sri Lankan girls was described in terms of dishonesty (e.g., lying to parents), stubbornness, not following etiquette, and engaging in romantic relationships or love affairs. Furthermore, girls did not approve of cross-gender behavior. They indicated that "girls who act or speak like boys or dress like boys" have behavioral problems. Males described the construct in different terms. They focused on behaviors such as delinquency (e.g., substance abuse, stealing, running away from home, joining gangs) and aggression (e.g., fighting, quarreling with adults or peers, assaulting others).

Personal/Interpersonal Needs

Students provided information about personal and interpersonal needs during their interviews. Although few gender differences were found in terms of this construct, it is does provide an interesting perspective of some of the pressures adolescents report. Respondents indicated that poverty limits their access to basic necessities of life such as proper food, clothing, housing and education. They also indicated that family support, both material and emotional, was very important for them to thrive. Meanwhile, several respondents, particularly girls, indicated that many mothers leave to work in the Middle East (e.g., Saudi Arabia, Jordan, Kuwait, Qatar, United Arab Emirates) for financial reasons. They find jobs as household workers or maids and send money to their families in Sri Lanka, leaving children to assume several domestic responsibilities without maternal support.

Respondents were vocal about their academic needs in terms of instructional support, guidance, and emotional support that they received from parents, teachers, peers, relatives, and private tutors. They particularly emphasized the importance of effective teaching in the classroom and the support from teachers to meet their academic needs (recall Sri

Lanka uses a high stakes examination system). They also described the lack of mental health services in school. They indicated that such services were only available through psychiatric centers at hospitals, which are often not readily accessible. Furthermore, mental illness is stigmatized in the culture and this is thought to reduce the likelihood that services will be accessed.

Respondents spoke about their need for extracurricular activities. In particular, they expressed the need for recreation and complained about lack of recreational opportunities due to academic pressure from parents. Sample quotes include:

> [Our] worst stress is tuition [private tutoring; additional instruction outside of the school context] . . . here all girls get tuition. We finish school at 2 p.m. and go home and grab a snack and go to tuition [meaning class] . . . we need other things like sports. But we don't have the time. [Female respondent]

> [There is] so much competition. We don't have lots of time to do extracurricular activities. There is not time to do things kids are supposed to do. No hobbies. We do not have time to do such things . . . we have little time, we get tired from going to classes. [Male respondent]

Students expressed a desire to go out with their friends, party, go on vacations, and watch sports and television. Interview data from adolescents and adults indicated that indulging in recreational activities is typically not permitted by parents because of the strong emphasis on academic preparation.

Several students mentioned interest in interacting with opposite-sex friends; meanwhile, Sri Lankan society does not encourage free interaction of males and females. For example, boys and girls mentioned that they were not allowed by their parents to interact with the opposite gender or have any relationship with them. Many students thought that this practice needs to be changed. They also indicated the importance of romantic relationships during adolescence and how their parents, relatives and the society did not approve of such relationships. Female respondents also indicated the lack of freedom and independence for girls in Sri Lankan society. They suggested that girls enjoyed much less freedom and independence in contrast with the boys. Their activities were restricted and supervised by parents and other elders. The girls expressed the need for more freedom and removal of restrictions that would allow them to function independently and would promote self-efficacy and self-confidence in girls.

Although adults emphasized the importance of suitable and unsuitable behaviors as critical to definitions of culturally-valued competencies, adolescents also emphasized behaviors that related to their personal and interpersonal needs. For this reason, when developing the perceived competence instrument, we included items related to effective engagement in recreational activities and interpersonal relationships (i.e., reflecting a more "well-rounded" adolescent or, as described in the culture, the "all-rounder").

FINDINGS FROM QUANTITATIVE ANALYSES

Principal Components Analysis (PCA). Recall that qualitative data were used to develop surveys. Analysis of survey responses yielded an initial scale structure that was congruent with the qualitative findings. Three factors were identified. *Unsuitable Behavior (socially unacceptable behavior)* [$\alpha = .94$; $\alpha = .95$ *(Female)*; $\alpha = .93$ *(Male)*] consisted of fifteen items (see Table 2). These items described behaviors viewed to be inappropriate within this culture (e.g., drug use, stealing, and fighting). *Suitable Behavior* (socially acceptable behavior) [$\alpha = .76$; $\alpha = .72$ *(Female)*; $\alpha = .78$ *(Male)*] consisted of thirteen items. This scale described desirable adolescent behaviors within this culture, including studying, following school rules, and remaining clean in appearance. The final factor, *Personal/Interpersonal Needs* (i.e., behaviors/competencies related to fulfilling personal and social needs of Sri Lankan adolescents) [$\alpha = .72$; $\alpha = .67$ *(Female)*; $\alpha = .76$ *(Male)*], consisted of nine items that described behaviors/competencies for meeting these needs. These needs included spending the day with friends and going to parties. These factor structures were expected both because of the qualitative analyses but also because they have been previously established with a similar survey (student perceptions of the degree to which parents value the behaviors) using the same sample (Hitchcock et al., 2005). Note, however, that the previous work did not examine the data for gender differences. Table 2 contains factor loadings for males and females as well as for the total sample.

MANOVA analyses were performed to test for gender differences. In the first MANOVA, gender was used as the independent variable, and the three scale scores were used as dependent variables. The overall MANOVA was significant, Wilks Lamdba = .96, $F(3, 606) = 8.77$, $p <$

TABLE 2. Factor Loadings Resulting from Principal Components Analysis (PCA) and Differences of Scale Scores and Individual Items by Gender

Scale/Item	Factor Loadings			Overall	Male	Female
	Overall	Female	Male	Mean (SE)	Mean(SE)	Mean(SE)
Suitable Behaviors Cronbach Alpha(α)	.94	.95	.93	2.75 (.23)	2.70 (.25)	2.79 (19)***
I am honest.	.62	.59	.61	2.81 (.41)	2.75 (.45)	2.87 (.35)***
I obey school and classroom rules.	.60	.54	.60	2.87 (.35)	2.80 (.42)	2.92 (.26)***
When somebody shows me a mistake, I like to accept it and correct myself.	.58	.45	.64	2.84 (.38)	2.77 (.44)	2.90 (.31)***
I like to look after others who are sick or hurt.	.57	.54	.53	2.73 (.47)	2.64 (.53)	2.83 (.39)***
I study regularly.	.55	.53	.55	2.58 (.51)	2.53 (.53)	2.64 (.49)**
I pay attention to the studies in the school.	.55	.49	.60	2.94 (.24)	2.92 (.27)	2.95 (.21)
I persevere even when faced with a difficult task.	.48	.48	.63	2.66 (.52)	2.60 (.56)	2.72 (.47)**
I help the poor through good works.	.47	.45	.44	2.62 (.49)	2.53 (.51)	2.70 (.46)***
I interact well with my teachers.	.47	.48	.46	2.85 (.37)	2.83 (.40)	2.88 (.35)
I move with respectable peers.	.45	.31	.55	2.72 (.53)	2.68 (.56)	2.75 (.51)
I follow rules and expectations according to the situation.	.44	.41	.44	2.83 (.39)	2.80 (.42)	2.85 (.37)
I observe customs and traditions of the country.	.43	.52	.43	2.71 (.47)	2.67 (.49)	2.75 (.43)*
I am clever (intelligent).	.42	.47	.37	2.63 (.50)	2.67 (.50)	2.60 (.50)
Unsuitable Behaviors Cronbach Alpha (α)	.76	.72	.78	1.06 (.22)	1.08 (.23)	1.05 (.21)
I use drugs.	.91	.92	.91	1.03 (.21)	1.04 (.23)	1.02 (.20)
I drink alcohol.	.91	.94	.89	1.03 (.23)	1.04 (.24)	1.03 (.23)
I steal.	.90	.94	.86	1.03 (.23)	1.04 (.24)	1.03 (.23)
I carry weapons.	.85	.93	.75	1.04 (.26)	1.06 (.27)	1.04 (.25)
I smoke cigarettes.	.85	.89	.81	1.03 (.23)	1.03 (.25)	1.03 (.22)
I persuade others to join a gang.	.82	.84	.81	1.03 (.24)	1.03 (.25)	1.03 (.24)

TABLE 2 (continued)

Scale/Item	Factor Loadings Overall	Female	Male	Overall Mean (SE)	Male Mean(SE)	Female Mean(SE)
Unsuitable Behaviors Cronbach Alpha(α)	.76	.72	.78	1.06 (.22)	1.08 (.23)	1.05 (.21)
I persuade others to engage in bad habits.	.79	.75	.83	1.04 (.25)	1.04 (.25)	1.03 (.24)
I insult others.	.73	.86	.59	1.09 (.32)	1.12 (.35)	1.05 (.29)
I use profane language	.71	.77	.68	1.09 (.33)	1.13 (.28)	1.05 (.27)
I scold or criticize teachers.	.72	.80	.65	1.09 (.33)	1.13 (.38)	1.06 (.27)
I interrupt others' work.	.72	.74	.70	1.09 (.23)	1.10 (.23)	1.07 (.23)
I associate with bad peers.	.69	.86	.57	1.08 (.31)	1.14 (.37)	1.04 (.23)
I am a member of a gang.	.70	.71	.71	1.07 (.32)	1.06 (.28)	1.07 (.35)
I waste time.	.60	.57	.64	1.10 (.37)	1.12 (.40)	1.08 (.34)
I don't carry out my responsibilities.	.45	.53	.36	1.17 (.46)	1.17 (.46)	1.17 (.29)
Personal/Interpersonal Needs Cronbach Alpha (α)	.72	.67	.76	2.50 (.34)	2.48 (.36)	2.52 (.31)
I like to spend the day with friends.	.69	.65	.71	2.42 (.63)	2.38 (.65)	2.46 (.62)
I like to have fun with others.	.62	.61	.64	2.56 (.59)	2.56 (.59)	2.56 (.60)
I listen to others' problems.	.61	.48	.70	2.21 (.76)	2.19 (.74)	2.22 (.77)
I like to listen to music or sing.	.53	.50	.55	2.70 (.49)	2.65 (.51)	2.75 (.46)
I like to go on trips.	.53	.54	.53	2.64 (.53)	2.67 (.53)	2.61 (.53)
I help others to solve their problems.	.49	.41	.53	2.55 (.57)	2.52 (.60)	2.58 (.55)
I am sensitive to others' feelings and needs.	.48	.40	.49	2.41 (.59)	2.39 (.59)	2.43 (.60)
I like to go to parties.	.49	.49		2.40 (.58)	2.42 (.61)	2.39 (.55)
I safeguard others' secrets.	.40	.41	.40	2.61 (.64)	2.54 (.66)	2.67 (.63)

Note: * $p < .05$; ** $p < .01$; *** $p < .001$

.001. The follow-up analysis indicated that one of the scales, *Suitable Behaviors*, was different by gender [$F(3,606) = 25.3$, $p < .001$], with girls scoring higher than boys. The other two factors were not statistically significant at the .05 level (*Unsuitable Behaviors*–$F(3,606) = 3.07$, $p = .08$; *Personal/Interpersonal Needs*–$F(3,606) = 2.45$, $p = .12$). Subsequent analyses were performed to examine the individual items in the *Suitable Behaviors* factor by gender. The overall MANOVA, as expected, was statistically significant (Wilks Lamdba = .90, $F(13, 582) = 4.80$, $p < .001$). Table 2 contains more detailed information of the analysis, including the items in each factor, the factor loading on the individual factor, the means and standard errors for each factor and item by gender, and significant differences (determined by the MANOVA) by gender. To summarize, results of the factor analyses provided construct validation of perceived competencies consistent with cultural concepts reflected in the qualitative data. A key finding is that the suitable behavior construct differs by gender; in general, girls reported more suitable behaviors.

Examination of the factor loadings for boys and for girls indicated that there might be differences in factor structure. Such differences can illuminate ways in which boys and girls interpret items within a construct differently. Tests for factor (construct) invariance using structural equation modeling can be used to help locate such statistical differences that can then be compared to qualitative findings (see Byrne, 1994). Hypotheses are developed that test the equivalence of factor loadings across groups (levels of gender, in this case). While the details of the analysis are beyond the scope of this paper, we conducted preliminary analyses using this technique.[1] Table 3 contains a summary of the analyses. The strategy is to initially test the equivalence of the factor structure across groups; then, successively restrictive equality constraints are imposed on the models. For example, the constraints of interest here are the factors loadings. If item factor loadings are constrained to be equal across models, and the change in the degrees of freedom and chi-square are examined, a statistically significant chi-square statistic suggests differences in structure. The results of Table 3 show that, while *Suitable Behaviors* and *Personal & Interpersonal Needs* factor items load equivalently for boys and girls, there are differences in the factor structure of *Unsuitable Behaviors*.

This finding is supported by the qualitative data which indicated that several behaviors such as joining gangs, robbing, carrying weapons, assaulting people, alcohol and drug abuse were described only by male respondents and viewed as only relevant to males. This occurrence may

TABLE 3. Constrained Models CFA Tests Summary of Analyses

Model	χ^2	Df	$\Delta\chi^2$	Δdf	CFI	RMSEA
Full, 3 Factor Model, no constraints	4246.637	1252			.964	.06
Full, 3 Factor Model, Factor loadings, variance, covariances constrained to be equal	4493.456	1326	246.82	74*	.962	.06
Full, 3 Factor Model, Factor loadings only for all three factors constrained	4334.142	1286	87.51	34*	.963	.06
Unsuitable Behaviors only constrained	4306.790	1266	60.15	14*	.963	.06
Suitable Behaviors only constrained	4265.249	1264	18.62	12	.964	.06
P & IP Needs only constrained	4255.381	1260	8.744	8	.964	.06

$^*p < .05$
Note. Models were compared to the full models with no constraints. The results suggest (and are consistent with exploratory analysis) that structures for Unsuitable Behaviors are different for boys and girls.

be explained by the cultural emphasis on gender-appropriate behavior which is comparatively more rigid and less permissive for women. Some caution is needed to avoid over-interpretation. The assessment tool used for quantitative data collection was a self-report instrument and the female respondents may have included only the socially desirable responses to conform to the cultural expectations. These differences in definition and interpretation of unsuitable behavior do, however, require further examination.

DISCUSSION

When dealing with populations with distinct cultural variables, researchers typically employ preexisting clinical or research instruments developed for mainstream American children and adolescents, in some instances with minimal modifications (e.g., language translation) and without re-validation. This is problematic because of the likelihood that such instruments will miss nuanced issues important to a target population. The work described here provides an alternative and represents theoretical and methodological approaches for investigating the role of individual and cultural factors in mental health of a distinct culture, particularly the combined use of ethnographic and factor analytic techniques. As a result of this effort, a culturally specific instrument that measures self-concept issues in Sri Lanka was developed and yielded insights into the culture. There is compelling data that show girls report that they endeavor to follow societal expectations for culturally-defined suitable behavior when compared to boys. This could be attributed to the cultural emphasis on a traditional gender role behavior that encourages submissiveness, tolerance and a caring attitude in women (Das Dasgupta, 1996).

The findings dealing with girls' perceptions of suitable and unsuitable behavior may prove useful when engaged in future work in the culture. Should a girl appear to not be following expectations, we can now recognize that follow-up may be important. The girl may simply be unusually independent, or she might be reacting to some difficult life circumstances. Whatever the case, these analyses provide a basis for recognizing the behavior as unusual and follow-up may be warranted. This work also suggests a need to revisit the unsuitable behavior construct in light of gender-specificity. As noted above, the items that form the factor structure for the construct load differently by gender. This is a subtle difference from the MANOVA results indicating differences in suitable behavior. In this latter construct, the data do not suggest the genders define the construct differently; girls simply scored higher than boys. For Unsuitable Behavior, however, Table 2 shows the factor loadings for some items were higher for girls than boys (e.g., I carry weapons, I insult others, I scold or criticize others, I associate with bad peers, and I don't carry out my responsibilities). This suggests greater variability in how males responded to these items and the issue can be further explored in future studies. The Personal/Interpersonal Needs construct appeared in the factor analysis, but this was not gender-specific. These findings were congruent with qualitative data; there was no reason to suspect there would be gender differences on this factor. The identification of this third factor can also inform future intervention work. The data suggest that Sri Lankan students recognize a need for recreational time with friends, yet this is generally not allowed by parents and educators. Communicating this finding to stakeholders may alone be beneficial as allowing for more recreation may reduce stress among adolescents (a long-term goal of this research program). More generally, the psychological constructs presented here have been validated by qualitative and factor analytic data analyses, so researchers can proceed with confidence using this instrument for wider research projects within the country.

One limitation of the present study is that our data did not completely capture indicators of socioeconomic status (SES); qualitative work did not highlight this as an important factor. Ancillary analyses (not shown) including mother and father education as SES indicators as covariates did not change any of the conclusions made here, and gender did not interact with SES variables. However, the results of those analyses suggested that SES indicators may offer important ways to understand elements of students' self-concept in Sri Lanka; this issue should be explored in future research.

We opened with a discussion as to why having knowledge of a target culture facilitates assessment. A specific example was provided using Old Order Amish and the data here further demonstrate the point. Now suppose that, in Sri Lanka, an interventionist meets a girl who reports she is rejecting behavior expectations imposed upon her by parents by actively seeking out recreational activity in lieu of studying and engaging in cross-gender behavior (e.g., acting or dressing like a boy). In the United States this behavior would not be considered unusual and possibly even be encouraged; in Sri Lanka, such behavior would be non-normative and a caregiver would do well to pay closer attention to the girl's circumstances. This raises the issue of whether it is better to change the local culture to facilitate such independence or to get the girls to conform. This represents a complex debate, but the importance of intervening on the girl's behalf at some level would be clear and the caregiver should not dismiss the behavior. The point is that, as with the case of the Old Order Amish, knowledge of cultural variation would solicit very different behaviors among practitioners. In other words, detailed knowledge of a culture facilitates assessment and the development of sensitive interventions, which is very much in-line with calls for developing cultural competency. As a side note, we have confidence in these findings because there is cross-method consistency (i.e., triangulation) that supports their validity. In-depth qualitative findings, obtained from smaller groups, were consistent with the results of the various quantitative analyses described above, using a large sample.

Finally, these findings should not be of interest only to those with interests in mixed-methods and cross-cultural work; there are implications here for school psychologists. Psychologists are being pushed to develop cultural competencies and the methods described above support this endeavor. When working in a multicultural setting, the qualitative procedures can serve as models for service planning and identifying relevant cultural issues, and the development of a survey from this information can be used to quantify such information in the event a large enough sample warrants the additional effort. These skills can help school psychologists understand the idiosyncratic needs of a local culture, develop nuanced assessment skills and in turn develop highly targeted interventions.

NOTE

1. More detailed findings can be obtained from the first author.

REFERENCES

American Psychological Association (1990). *Guidelines for providers of psychological services to ethnic, linguistic, and culturally diverse populations.* Washington, DC: Author.

American Psychological Association (2003). Guidelines on multicultural education, training, research, practice, and organizational change for psychologists. *American Psychologist, 58,* 377-402.

Anshel, M. H., Porter, A., & Quek, J. (1998). Coping with acute stress in sport as a function of gender: An exploratory study. *Journal of Sport Behavior, 21 (4),* 363-376.

Baxter, J. (1998). Culture and Women's Mental Health: International Perspectives and Issues for Aotearoa/New Zealand. In Sarah Romans (ed.) *Folding Back the Shadows: A Perspective on Women's Mental Health.* Dunedin, NZ: University of Otago Press.

Bird, G. W., & Harris, R. L. (1990). A comparison of role strain and coping strategies by gender and family structure among early adolescents. *Journal of Early Adolescents, 10,* 141-158.

Block, J., & Robins, R. W. (1993). A longitudinal study of consistency and change in self-esteem from early adolescence to early adulthood. *Child Development, 64,* 909-923.

Brannon, L. (2002). *Gender: Psychological Perspectives* (3rd ed.). Boston: Allyn and Bacon.

Bronfenbrenner, U. (1989). Ecological systems theory. In R. Vasta (Ed.), *Annals of Child Development* (Vol. 6, pp. 187-249). Greenwich, CT: JAI Press.

Bronfenbrenner, U. (1999). Environments in developmental perspective: Theoretical and operational models. In S. L. Friedman & T. D. Wachs (Eds.), *Measuring environment across the life span: Emerging methods and concepts* (pp. 3-30).Washington, DC: American Psychological Association.

Byrne, B.M. (1994). *Structural equation modeling with EQS and EQS/Windows: Basic concepts, applications and programming.* Thousand Oaks, CA: Sage.

Castillo, R.J. (1997). *Culture and Mental Illness: A Client-Centered Approach.* Pacific Grove, CA: Brooks-Cole.

Das, A. K., & Kemp, S. F. (1997). Between two worlds: Counseling South Asian Americans. *Journal of Multicultural Counseling and Development, 25 (1),* 23-33.

Das Dasgupta, S. (1996). Feminist consciousness in women-centered Hindi films. *Journal of Popular Culture, 30 (1),* 173-189.

Egeland, J.A., Hostetter, A.M., & Eshleman, S.K. (1983). Amish study III: The impact of cultural factors on diagnosis of bipolar illness. *American Journal of Psychiatry, 140*, 67-71.

Elias, M. J. & Branden, L. R. (1988). Primary prevention of behavioral and emotional problems in school-aged populations. *School Psychology Review, 17*, 581-592.

Frydenberg, E. (2002). (Ed.). *Beyond coping: Meeting goals, visions, and challenges.* Oxford, UK: Oxford University Press.

Gunaratna, R. (1990). *Sri Lanka: A Lost Revolution.* Kandy, Sri Lanka: Institute of Fundamental Studies.

Hall, G.C.N. & Okazaki, S. (2002). (Eds.). *Asian American Psychology: The science of lives in context.* Washington, DC: APA.

Harter, S. (1999). *The construction of the self: A developmental perspective.* New York: Guilford.

Henning-Stout, M. & Brown-Cheathem, M.A. (1999). School psychology in a diverse world: Considerations for practice, research, and teaching. In C.R. Reynolds & T.B. Gutkin (Eds.), *The handbook of school psychology, 3rd edition* (pp. 1041-1055). New York: John Wiley & Sons Inc.

Hitchcock, J. H., Nastasi, B. K., Dai, D. Y., Newman, J., Jayasena, A., Bernstein-Moore, R., Sarkar, S., & Varjas, K. (2005). Illustrating a mixed-method approach for validating culturally specific constructs. *Journal of School Psychology, 43*, 259-278.

Knox, M., Funk, J., Elliott, R., & Bush, E. G. (1998). Adolescents' possible selves and their relationship to global self-esteem. *Sex Roles, 39 (1/2)*, 61-80.

Lazarus, R. S., & Folkman, S. (1984). *Stress, appraisal, and coping.* New York: Springer.

Nastasi, B. K., & DeZolt, D. M. (1994). *School interventions for children of alcoholics.* New York: Guilford.

Nastasi, B. K., Varjas, K., Sarkar, S., & Jayasena, A. (1998). Participatory model of mental health programming: Lessons learned from work in a developing country. *School Psychology Review, 27*, 260-276.

Nastasi, B. K., Varjas, K., Jayasena, A., Bernstein Moore, R., Sarkar, S., Hitchcock, J., & Burkholder, G. (2005). *Sri Lanka mental health promotion project.* Unpublished manuscript. Minneapolis, MN: Walden University School of Psychology.

Nastasi, B.K., Moore, R. B., & Varjas, K. M. (2004). *School-Based Mental Health Services: Creating Comprehensive and Culturally Specific Programs.* Washington, DC: American Psychological Association.

Padilla, A.M. (2001). Issues in culturally appropriate assessment. On L.A. Suzuki, J.G. Ponterotto, & P.J. Meller (Eds.), *Handbook of multicultural assessment*, 2nd edition, (pp. 5-27). San Francisco: Jossey-Bass.

Ptacek, J. T., Smith, R. E., & Dodge, K. L. (1994). Gender differences in coping with stress: When stressors and appraisal do not differ. *Personality and Social Psychology Bulletin, 20*, 421-430.

Rogers, M. R., Ingraham, C. L., Bursztyn, A., Cajigas-Segredo, N., Esquivel, G., Hess, R. S., & Nahari, S. G., & Lopez, E. C. (1999). Best practices in providing psychological services to racially, ethnically, culturally, and linguistically diverse individuals in the schools. *School Psychology International, 20*, 243-264.

Rogler, L.H. (1999). Methodological sources of cultural insensitivity in mental health research. *American Psychologist, 54*, 424-433.

Romans, S. E. (1998). Undertaking research with women. In S. E. Romans (Ed.), *Folding Back the Shadows: A Perspective on Women's Mental Health*, (pp. 23-34). Dunedin, NZ: University of Otago Press.

Sarkar, S. (2003). *Gender as a cultural factor influencing mental health among the adolescent students in India and Sri Lanka: A cross-cultural study.* Unpublished doctoral dissertation. University at Albany, State University of New York, Albany.

Schensul, J. J., & LeCompte, M. D. (1999). *Ethnographer's Toolkit* (Volumes 1-7). Walnut Creek, CA: AltaMira.

Snyder, C. R., & Lopez, S. J. (2002). (Eds.). *Handbook of positive psychology.* Oxford, UK: Oxford University.

Sue, D. W., Bingham, R. P., Porche-Burke, L., & Vasquez, M. (1999). The diversification of psychology: A multicultural revolution. *American Psychologist, 54,* 1061-1069.

Tanaka, J. S., Ebreo, A., Linn, N., & Morera, O. F. (1998). Research methods: The construct validity of self-identity and its psychological implications. In L. C. Lee & N. W. S. Zane (Eds.), *Handbook of Asian American Psychology* (pp. 21-82). Thousand Oaks, CA: Sage.

Tashakkori, A. & Teddlie, C. (2003). *Handbook of mixed methods in social and behavioral research.* Sage: Thousand Oaks, CA: Sage.

The World Bank in Sri Lanka (April 2003). *The World Development Indicator Database.* Retrieved April 16, 2003, from the World Bank in Sri Lanka website; http://lnweb18.worldbank.org/sar/sa.nsf/srilanka

United Nations Development Programme (2002). *Human Development Indicators, 2002.* Retrieved on April 17, 2003. http://hdr.undp.org/reports/global/2002/en/indicator/indicator.cfm?File=index.html.

U.S. Department of Health and Human Services (1999). *Mental health: A report of the Surgeon General.* Rockville, MD: U.S. Department of Health and Human Services, Substance Abuse and Mental Health Administration, Center for Mental Health Services, National Institutes of Health, National Institute of Mental Health.

U.S. Department of Health and Human Services (2001). *Mental health: Culture, race, and ethnicity–A supplement to mental health: A report of the Surgeon General.* Rockville, MD: U.S. Department of Health and Human Services, Substance Abuse and Mental Health Administration, Center for Mental Health Services.

doi:10.1300/J370v22n02_02

Using a Participatory Culture-Specific Intervention Model to Develop a Peer Victimization Intervention

Kris Varjas
Joel Meyers
Christopher C. Henrich
Emily C. Graybill
Brian J. Dew
Megan L. Marshall
Zachary Williamson
Rebecca B. Skoczylas

Georgia State University

Marty Avant

City Schools of Decatur, Decatur, GA

SUMMARY. The purpose of the Peer Victimization Intervention (PVI) was to develop and implement a culture-specific pilot intervention to address the effects of bullying on middle school students who are victims

Address correspondence to: Kris Varjas, Counseling and Psychological Services, P.O. Box 3980, Atlanta, GA 30302-3980 (E-mail: kvarjas@gsu.edu).

[Haworth co-indexing entry note]: "Using a Participatory Culture-Specific Intervention Model to Develop a Peer Victimization Intervention." Varjas, Kris et al. Co-published simultaneously in *Journal of Applied School Psychology* (The Haworth Press, Inc.) Vol. 22, No. 2, 2006, pp. 35-57; and: *Multicultural Issues in School Psychology* (ed: Bonnie K. Nastasi) The Haworth Press, Inc., 2006, pp. 35-57. Single or multiple copies of this article are available for a fee from The Haworth Document Delivery Service [1-800-HAWORTH, 9:00 a.m. - 5:00 p.m. (EST). E-mail address: docdelivery@haworthpress.com].

utilizing the Participatory Culture-Specific Intervention Model (PCSIM; Nastasi, Moore, & Varjas, 2004). The involvement of participants who serve as cultural brokers in the system and/or stakeholders was used to encourage acceptability, integrity, ecological validity, sustainability, and institutionalization of the intervention. The pilot intervention was conducted in an urban, multiethnic school system and implemented during the school day by a multidisciplinary team of service providers. Twenty-eight students (11 sixth graders, 13 seventh graders, 4 eighth graders) participated in a 6-session pilot intervention group. Qualitative and quantitative data were collected from the students and co-facilitators of each group to assess acceptability, integrity, and efficacy. Quantitative pilot data indicated that levels of post-traumatic stress symptoms decreased from pre-test to post-test. Qualitative data provided information about students' perceptions of reasons for bullying, characteristics of bullies and victims, student and adult responses to bullying, and places where bullying incidents occur. Qualitative findings also indicated a high degree of intervention acceptability and integrity. doi:10.1300/J370v22n02_03 *[Article copies available for a fee from The Haworth Document Delivery Service: 1-800-HAWORTH. E-mail address: <docdelivery@haworthpress.com> Website: <http://www.HaworthPress.com>* © 2006 by The Haworth Press, Inc. All rights reserved.]

KEYWORDS. Collaborative consultation, harassment, school intervention, participation, culture

The call for expanding the role of the practicing school psychologist has resonated in the literature for over thirty years (e.g., Furlong, Morrison, & Pavelski, 2000; Gutkin & Conoley, 1990). One focus for role expansion is the involvement of school psychologists in the development, implementation, and evaluation of prevention and intervention to address individual, cultural, and contextual needs in schools (e.g., Furlong, Morrison, & Pavelski, 2000; Leff, Power, Manz, Cogstigan, & Nabors, 2001; Nastasi, 1998; Nastasi, Moore, & Varjas, 2004; Sheridan & Gutkin, 2000; Varjas, Nastasi, Moore, & Jayasena, 2005).

One pragmatic approach to role expansion is to develop culture-specific interventions that have several potential advantages such as ensuring cultural specificity, while increasing acceptability, integrity, ecological validity, sustainability, and institutionalization of interventions (Nastasi, Varjas, Bernstein, & Jayasena, 2000). Participatory research has been proposed as an approach to develop, implement and evaluate culture-specific interventions (e.g., Ho, 2002; Leff et al., 2001; Nastasi et al., 2004; Vastine & Anliker, 2005). Culturally sensitive research requires that cultural and contextual issues are addressed at every phase of the research process through the participation of stakeholders (e.g., Dumas, Rollack, Prinz, Hops, & Blechman, 1999; Nastasi et al., 2004). School psychologists are in a unique position to facilitate mental health service delivery by developing partnerships with school personnel, students, parents, and community members (e.g., Ho, 2002; Leff, Power, Costigan, & Manz, 2003).

PARTICIPATORY CULTURE-SPECIFIC INTERVENTION MODEL (PCSIM)

This research project, Reducing Bullying in an Urban School District (RBUSD), utilizes the Participatory Culture-Specific Intervention Model (PCSIM; see Nastasi et al., 2004 for a detailed description) as a framework to study and intervene to reduce school-based bullying. This model requires active participation of stakeholders in interpreting evidence, and designing, implementing, and evaluating interventions. PCSIM enhances acceptability, social validity, treatment integrity/fidelity, efficacy, sustainability and institutionalization (Nastasi et al., 2004). Within PCSIM, *culture* is defined as the shared language, ideas, beliefs, values, and behavioral norms of the members of the culture; and *culture specificity* is defined as reflecting both the real-life experiences of the cultural group and the individual interpretations of those experiences (Nastasi et al., 1998). PCSIM is an 11-phase model that guides program development starting with systems entry and ending with program continuation or extension (Nastasi et al., 2004). The formative research component encompasses Phases 1 through 6, and Phases 7 through 11 comprise the intervention component.

The *formative research component* begins with Existing Theory, Research, and Practice (Phase 1), which requires that the researcher makes explicit and/or develops his/her own personal theory, based on experiences and scientific literature, which will guide the work in subsequent phases. Learning the Culture (Phase 2) involves efforts to understand the cultural experiences of the stakeholders. Forming Partnerships (Phase 3) involves establishing relationships between researchers and stakeholders in order to enhance culture specificity of the intervention. During Phase 3, the researcher identifies cultural brokers (i.e., individuals who are members of the identified culture and facilitate system entry, acceptance, and interpretation) and initiates active involvement of participants. Partnership efforts continue through subsequent phases. During Goal/Problem Identification (Phase 4), partners identify what is going to be investigated in their setting. Formative Research (Phase 5) involves the partners in data collection to obtain an in-depth understanding of the target problem and context. Based on formative research data and personal theory, a Culture-Specific Theory/Model (Phase 6) is proposed to explain the target phenomena (e.g., bullying) and guide development of the intervention.

The *intervention component* begins with the process of development (Phase 7), implementation (Phase 8), and evaluation of the intervention (Phase 9) as researchers and stakeholders work together to create a culture-specific program. In the PCSIM, particular attention is given not only to evaluating intervention effectiveness, but also to evaluating intervention acceptability, social validity and integrity (Nastasi et al., 2004). Capacity Building (Phase 10) ensures that researchers and stakeholders develop plans to sustain and institutionalize research efforts. The final stage involves translation (Phase 11) of the research through dissemination and deployment of the process and findings to other cultures and/or contexts.

This article focuses on application of the formative research component (Phases 1-5) of PCSIM to development and piloting of the Peer Victimization Intervention (PVI). The PVI was piloted in 2004-2005 as a sub-study within the larger Reducing Bullying in an Urban School District (RBUSD) project. Described herein are the process used to ensure culture specificity of the intervention and the evaluation of the pilot as part of the formative research process.

Rationale for Studying Bullying

Bullying and violence are growing problems in United States schools that affect most children. Bullying is defined as systematic, physical, and verbal aggression against an individual that is instigated by another individual or group of individuals (Espelage & Swearer, 2003; Olweus, 1993). Bullying is repeated behavior occurring over time in a relationship characterized by an imbalance of power and strength (Olweus). Reports from a substantial number of children about involvement in some aspect of bullying, recent events (e.g., Red Lake High School, Rocori High School), and recent research demonstrate that bullying is a major concern for students, school personnel, and parents (e.g., Nansel et al., 2001; Pellegrini, Bartini & Brooks, 1999; Stockdale, Hangaduambo, Duys, Larson & Sarvela, 2002).

Bullying has been associated with a range of physical symptoms such as stomachaches, poor sleep, sore throats, bed wetting, headaches, dizziness, backaches, and depression (Forero, McLellan, Rissel, & Bauman, 1999; Wolke, Woods, Bloomfield, & Karstadt, 2001). Many children victimized by bullies have reported mental health symptoms, including increased anxiety (Slee, 1994), antisocial behavior and depression (Roland, 2002; Snyder et al., 2003), low self-esteem (Salmon, James, & Smith, 1998), and loneliness and suicidal ideations (e.g., Rivers, 2001; Roland, 2002). Children who are bullied often suffer negative academic consequences including academic failure and high absenteeism (Salmon, James, Cassidy, & Javaloyes, 2000; Slee, 1994) and many students report that school is not the safe place that many adults expect (Batsche & Knoff, 1994).

The purpose of the Peer Victimization Intervention (PVI) study was to develop and pilot a culture-specific intervention designed to address the effects of bullying on victims. The PVI focused specifically on the mental health of middle school victims of bullying. The intervention had three objectives: (a) to increase problem solving and coping skills of victims; (b) to increase victims' resources in the school and community; and (c) to increase victims' sense of belonging in school.

This article presents the implementation of a research-intervention process that occurred over time in an effort to influence the climate associated with bullying in one school system. This work illustrates how the PCSIM can be used to integrate qualitative and quantitative data collection, data analysis and feedback, in order to ensure development of a culture-specific intervention program (Nastasi et al., 2004).

METHODOLOGY

The methodology specific to the application of Phases 1 through 5 (formative research components of PCSIM) to development and piloting of the PVI is presented in this section. The study context, participants, and procedures relevant to each phase are described.

Phase 1. Existing Theory, Research, and Practice. Phase 1 requires researchers to identify the theory that will guide their work. For the purposes of this study, we adopted the Ecological-Developmental Model of Mental Health (EDMMH; Nastasi et al., 2005) as the conceptual framework for investigating individual and cultural factors related to the mental health of the targeted youth. The EDMMH has foundations in psychology and anthropology and has been used in prior work by the first author and colleagues in the U.S., Sri Lanka, and India (Nastasi et al., 2004; Nastasi & DeZolt, 1994; Nastasi et al., 1998; Nastasi et al., 1998-99). The EDMMH conceptualizes individual mental health, in part, as an interaction among personal factors, including self-perceptions of culturally valued competencies, personal resources, and personal vulnerability.

A major assumption of EDMMH is that the relationship between individual and cultural factors influences psychological functioning and mental health. The model incorporates an ecological-developmental framework (Bronfenbrenner, 1989) that considers (a) risk and protective factors related to mental health/illness of individuals as well as community prevalence (e.g., Elias & Branden, 1988), (b) models of stress and coping (e.g., Lazarus & Folkman, 1984), and (c) models of personal-social competence (e.g., Nastasi & DeZolt, 1994). Furthermore, the documented role of key ecological contexts of family, peer group, school, community, and society in promoting the psychological development and mental health of children and adolescents necessitates an ecological perspective (Nastasi et al., 2004; Varjas, 2003). The EDMMH provided the conceptual framework for the systematic study of bullying and the role of contextual, social, cultural and historical factors on the mental health and psychological well-being of adolescents.

Phase 2. Learning the Culture. Phase 2 activities in the current project included qualitative and quantitative data collection (e.g., key informant and in-depth interviews, participant observations) to examine the culture of the school, school district and community. The results provided a picture of the context in which the project would be developed. The project is currently in its third year of a planned long-term research collaboration involving a university and a metro-Atlanta school system.

The university has a history of placing school psychology students in practicum and internship at this district. The Director of Exceptional Student Services (ESS) was a school psychologist who served as a supervisor of the graduate students. Two specialist-level school psychology students were placed in the school system in 2004-2005 and three specialist-level students in 2005-2006. These students were assigned to the PVI as part of their placement requirements.

The Director of ESS initially approached two of the authors regarding the possibility of studying bullying in the school system, specifically bullying of gay, lesbian, bisexual, transgender, questioning, and intersex (GLBTQI) youth and ethnic minorities. A 7th grade middle school counselor had been conducting anti-bullying programs and had developed a discipline referral process to track bullying incidents and consequences for the bullies. The director and middle school counselor had conducted group interviews in the middle school in 2003-2004 to collect data regarding bullying incidents targeted toward GLBTQI youth and ethnic minorities. In addition, they had conducted diversity trainings for staff to address school climate and bullying related to sexual orientation and ethnic diversity. The school system held a town-hall meeting during the 2003-2004 school year to discuss the widespread concerns about bullying. The high school had a Gay Straight Alliance (GSA) that was reorganized in 2004-2005.

According to school personnel (personal communication, September 2004), bullying in the middle school was related to ethnicity, socioeconomic status (i.e., class), and perceived sexual orientation. School personnel also reported that bullying differed as a function of gender and grade level in the middle school; for example, the content (e.g., name calling, use of verbal versus physical attacks) of bullying differed by grade level.

Phase 3. Forming Partnerships. In Phase 3, researchers seek to form partnerships. Our research team developed not only school-based partnerships (e.g., school counselors, school psychologists), but also community-based partnerships in the metropolitan area surrounding the school district (e.g., organizations that support GLBTQI youth). Two key personnel were identified as cultural brokers (Director of ESS and 7th grade middle school counselor) and facilitated the research team's efforts to understand the system. They also identified key stakeholders and organized meetings.

Key stakeholders who participated in the project included the superintendent, assistant superintendent responsible for research, middle and 4th/5th grade school principals, middle school assistant principal, 4th/5th grade school counselor, middle school counselors, district service providers (e.g., social workers, behavior specialists, nurses), school board members, community members, community service providers (e.g., psychologists, counselors, agency directors, lawyers), parents, teachers, and students. Representatives of the research team presented information in the school district related to the project at PTA, school board, faculty, and staff development meetings. Finally, the RBSUD project sponsored two school staff members and one practicum student to attend the National Bullying Conference in 2004 and four school staff members and one doctoral student to attend the conference in 2005.

Phase 4. Goal/Problem Identification. During Phase 4, researchers and participants collaboratively identified contexts, foci, format, and content of interventions. This was accomplished through a series of meetings with stakeholders, where researchers presented preliminary findings and engaged participants in collaborative decision-making. Using a small group format, researchers and participants identified specific mental health needs and resources as a basis for developing action plans (long- and short-term) that guided the formative research and the development of a series of intervention activities.

Phase 5. Formative Research. Multiple data collection methods were used during this phase. Key informant interviews were conducted to gather information about bullying and GLBTQI issues. In-depth interviews with GLBTQI youth were focused on specific issues identified by school personnel and students. These interviews were conducted using recursive methods in which analysis of data collected early influenced the collection and analysis of data collected later. In-depth interviews also were conducted with students in the fourth through eighth grade to obtain their perspectives on bullying.

A major focus during the formative research phase for the larger RBUSD project was to develop, implement, and evaluate a culture-specific pilot bullying intervention for middle school students who are victims of bullying. The pilot intervention (PVI) and its evaluation are described in the subsequent sections of this paper.

Participants

Participants in the pilot intervention included group members (middle school students) and group leaders (middle school and university staff). Each group is described separately. First, the context in which the pilot intervention was conducted is described.

Target School Context. The culture-specific intervention (PVI) was conducted at a middle school located within a small school district in metropolitan Atlanta. The school district consists of one preschool, three schools serving kindergarten through third-grade, one school serving fourth and fifth grades, one middle school serving sixth through eighth graders, and one high school. The school district's total enrollment was 2,450 students, with 570 of those students attending the middle school. The racial breakdown of the school district was as follows: 47.5% African American, 47.3% Caucasian, 2.8% Multiracial, 1.2% Asian American, and .9% Hispanic. The racial breakdown of the middle school was 52.2% African American, 45.8% Caucasian, 1.5% Asian, and .6% Hispanic. Within the district, 39% of students received free or reduced lunch, whereas 47% of students in the middle school received free or reduced lunch. The racial and socioeconomic diversity of the middle school was atypical for the metropolitan area, the state, and the entire Southeast. The school's distinct racial and economic diversity necessitated a participatory culturally specific approach to develop an acceptable and effective bullying intervention to meet its unique cultural needs.

Group Members. The group members (student participants) were identified as victims of bullying by the cultural broker (school counselor), school administrators, or parents. The students and/or parents were approached by the cultural broker who explained the intervention and assessed their interest in participating. Of the 31 students approached, one chose not to participate and two failed to obtain parental/guardian consent for participation. The remaining sample consisted of 28 students (11 sixth graders, 13 seventh graders, and 4 eighth graders). Each participating student completed a form providing his/her assent to participate. Five grade- and gender-specific groups (4 to 7 members each) were formed. Of the participating students, 53.6% were African American, 39.3% Caucasian, and 7.1% Asian American. Participants ranged in age from 11 to 14 years.

Group Leaders. Six group leaders participated in the intervention. The cultural broker, who was the seventh grade school counselor, chose to act as a consultant to the group leaders during the intervention rather than participate as a group leader. The group leaders consisted of three specialist-level school psychology graduate students (two female, one male), one female doctoral level school psychology professor, one female specialist-level school counselor intern, and one male school counselor. Of the participating group leaders, 83.3% were Caucasian and 16.7% African American. Two of the three school psychology students were completing academic requirements in the target district at the time of the intervention, and both had been involved in the current project for over a year prior to the start of the intervention. The school psychology professor was the principal investigator of the study, who had experience implementing school- and community-based interventions utilizing PCSIM. The school counselor intern attended another local university and was completing her internship. She also lived in the school district and had one child enrolled in the target school. The sixth-grade school counselor, who participated as a group leader, had been employed by the school district for two years. Each group was led by at least one person who was the same gender as the group members.

Group Sessions

The pilot PVI consisted of six sessions, implemented during the last nine weeks of the academic year. The group sessions occurred during the students' non-academic classes. Session topics included: group rules and expectations, self-efficacy, assessing students' perceptions of bullying, reviewing and applying the Second Step problem-solving model (Committee for Children, 1997) to bullying situations, emotion- and problem-focused coping, and identifying personal and school resources. The Second Step problem-solving model was included per request of the cultural broker who teaches all incoming sixth grade students this particular approach. Signs depicting the Second Step model are posted throughout the school (e.g., counseling offices, classrooms). Data collected from each session were reviewed and, when appropriate, infused into subsequent group sessions (e.g., including specific bullying situations and contexts for bullying) in an effort to increase the culture specificity of the curriculum.

Data Collection

The use of mixed methods to evaluate interventions is consistent with PCSIM and involves the use of multiple data collection techniques and sources to ensure credibility of the findings through triangulation (Lincoln & Guba, 1985). This concept of triangulation (i.e., multiple data sources and methods) has been recommended as best practices in school psychology (Nastasi, Varjas, Schensul et al., 2000). Several data collection methods were used in this project to evaluate the acceptability, integrity and outcomes of the pilot intervention. These included group interviews with students, collection of curriculum artifacts (permanent products resulting from session activities), self-reports from teachers and students, audiotaping of sessions, formal and informal communication with group leaders, and standardized measures of children's mental health and behavioral status.

Group Interviews. During the second PVI session, group interviews were conducted as a curricular activity. Students ($n = 25$) were asked to describe the nature and frequency of school bullying, and the children who were most likely to be bullied ($N = 25$). Group interviews were audiotaped and later transcribed by group leaders.

Curriculum Artifacts. During the majority of the sessions, group members completed worksheets or drawings. For example, during Session 4, students (*n* = 23) completed worksheets outlining their views on appropriate and inappropriate responses to bullying. During Session 6, group members (*n* = 22) outlined their bodies on large rolls of paper and wrote thoughts and feelings on their outlines related to their positive and negative views of themselves. These artifacts and others provided information about the students' responses to bullying and the emotional impact of bullying experiences. Analyzing individual worksheets and drawings provided information about each student's feelings and experiences, whereas analyzing the artifacts for the group as a whole provided information about the common types of bullying and responses that occurred in the respective school context.

Acceptability Measures. Intervention acceptability was measured during each session through group member and group leader evaluation and reflection forms. The group member evaluation form included four questions, two questions assessing students' feelings about the sessions and two questions assessing what they liked and disliked about session activities. The group leader reflection form requested information about perceived acceptability of the session by the leaders and students. In addition, group leaders provided feedback about the applicability of the session to the age, gender and ethnicities of group members (i.e., culture specificity). Finally, the leader reflection form included a self-evaluation of the leader's performance in the session.

Integrity Measures. Intervention integrity data were collected for each session. Data sources included group leader journals, session curriculum outlines, audiotapes of sessions, ongoing interviews of group leaders, weekly emails by group leaders to senior researcher, and student artifacts.

Outcome Measures. Participants completed two pre- and post-test measures, the Behavior Assessment System for Children, Second Edition (BASC-2; Reynolds & Kamphaus, 2004) and the revised version of the Child Self-Report Post Traumatic Stress Reaction Index (CPTS-RI; Pynoos et al., 1993). Pre-test measures were administered one to two weeks prior to the start of the intervention; post-tests were administered within three days after completion of the intervention. Pre- and post-testing were conducted by group leaders with individual students. All but one of the students in the intervention completed both pre-test and post-test measures (*n* = 27; 13 boys).

The BASC-2, composed of 139 to185 items (depending on student's age), is designed to assess emotions, behaviors, and self-perceptions. The BASC-2 utilizes a Likert-type 4-point rating scale ranging from "never" to "almost always." The measure takes approximately 30 minutes to complete. A *T* score of 70 or above is considered clinically significant. This self-report measure has high internal consistency (α = .89) and test-retest reliability (r = .91; Reynolds & Kamphaus, 2004).

The CPTS-RI is a 20-item scale designed to assess stress reaction symptoms in school-aged children and adolescents after exposure to a broad range of traumatic events (Geoenjian et al., 1995; Pynoos et al., 1993; Roussos et al., 2005). Items use a 5-point Likert scale ranging from "none" (0) to "most of the time" (4) to rate the frequency of symptoms. A sum score of 38 has been used in prior research as the cutoff for clinically high levels of post-traumatic stress symptoms (Goenjian et al., 1995; Roussos et al., 2005). The CPTS-RI is highly correlated with the DSM-based diagnosis of posttraumatic stress disorder (PTSD; Pynoos et al., 1993). The scale has high internal consistency (α = .92) and test-retest reliability (r = .84; Roussos et al., 2005). In the current study, the pre-test internal consistency was α = .86, and the post-test internal consistency was α = .87. For the purposes of this study, the internalizing problems, school problems, and personal adjustment *T* scores were used.

RESULTS

A mixed-method (qualitative-quantitative) approach to data analysis was employed. Quantitative pre- and post-test scores (BASC-2 and CPTS-RI) were compared statistically, using repeated measures analysis of variance, to assess change in functioning following participation in the intervention. Research team members independently analyzed the qualitative data (e.g., curriculum artifacts) using an inductive coding process to identify themes related to the participants' perceptions of reasons for bullying, characteristics of bullies and victims, student and adult responses to bullying, and places where bullying incidents occur. Thematic analyses by individual researchers were compared for consensus (i.e., interrater agreement), and cases reflecting outliers were discussed (i.e., negative case analysis). A team member then presented a summary of the team's findings to the cultural broker for feedback, interpretation, and confirmation (i.e., member checking). These procedures are consistent with methods for ensuring trustworthiness and credibility of qualitative data (Lincoln & Guba, 1985). Findings are presented separately for qualitative and quantitative measures.

Group Interviews

The students shared many of their own experiences of being bullied during the group interviews, in addition to sharing stories about other students being bullied. Three major themes emerged: (a) race as the basis for victimization (i.e., being targeted for bullying); (b) physical differences as basis for victimization; and (c) disappointment in adult responses to bullying incidents in school.

Race was a common reason cited by students for being bullied, a finding consistent with the original problem identified by the adult key stakeholders in Phase 4. One student gave an example of a student experiencing bullying because of race. "There's this boy in my class and a lot of kids call him 'white chocolate' because he is white but he acts black. So a lot of kids tell him, 'Why do you always have to act black?'" Another student shared her own story about race-related bullying. "They will tease you like, I've been called stuff a couple times like, they'll call me an Oreo like, because they say I'm black on the outside but white on the inside, because I don't discriminate against race. I'll be your friend no matter what color you are, and it's just a whole bunch of names that they call me."

Other students stated they were bullied because of physical differences (e.g., body size). One student stated: "I think that like, if something's wrong with their body. Like, if like . . . because I have an under bite, and then people just make fun of me. People doing like [sticks lower jaw out]." Another student reported ". . . the fatter kids. No matter how small or how tall, always the fatter kids [are bullied]." One of this student's peers agreed, "Yeah, we're a big target."

The students stated that they were not satisfied with teachers' responses to bullying. In response to the question, "What do the teachers do about bullying?" students provided the following answers. "Nothing" "They don't like. . . sometimes, they don't do anything. They say, 'Sit down' and 'I don't want to hear that.'" "One word: nothing." "They don't [do] anything once you tell them because they usually just think you're playing around, and they say, 'OK, just stop and do your work.'" "I mean, some teachers don't do it because they don't care about the students, like if they're really bad." "Well, they don't actually do nothing because all they do is send them to ISS [in-school suspension], but that don't do nothing."

Curriculum Artifacts

Through the curriculum artifacts (i.e., products of student's work during session activities), students provided their perceptions on why children were bullied and common student responses to bullying. Three themes emerged as reasons students were bullied: (a) perceived sexual orientation, (b) poor hygiene, and (c) being new to the school system. For example, in one activity an eighth grade girl stated the following: "It hurts my feelings when someone calls [me] a dyke." A seventh grade boy wrote in his bully story that other children call him gay slurs. Two students wrote about one student who was consistently bullied because of her poor hygiene. One of these students stated the following: "She is unclean and looks kind of funny, which is why people make fun of her. . . Lots of time during the school day people will call her names like *Stinka* and *Medusa*. People always talk behind her back, and she has a hard time making friends." Other students reported being bullied because they were new to school. Upon arriving to the new school, students reported being made fun of or having false rumors spread about them.

Children often did not respond to bullying in ways adults considered appropriate, such as telling a teacher or walking away. Many students reported that they and most of their peers responded to bullying in one of two ways, they seek revenge or they ignore the situation completely. The boys overwhelmingly believed that violence was the only effective solution to bullying. A few of the boys drew graphic pictures in which a bully received physical punishment for his/her actions. An eighth grade girl reported that if she were bullied, she would "try to fight back or say something negative about them or someone." When evaluating possible solutions while working through the problem-solving model during Session 3, several sixth grade boys stated that if telling a teacher and walking away from the bully did not stop the bullying they would "hit them [the bullies]."

The most common reason given for not responding appropriately to bullying was fear. Most students reportedly feared being perceived as "weak," as the following eighth grade girl explained: ". . . if you try to get a teacher to solve it then they mite (sic) think you're scared and want to bully you even more." An additional reason is that bystanders in a bullying situation feared being the next target. In response to a question about obstacles to responding to bullying, an eighth grade girl stated: "Standing alone at times. Fear of being the next one to be bullied, the odds." Another student stated that standing up to the bully could backfire if the bully knew personal information about you. This student said: "... if you've gotten in a verbal fight then it could backfire and get personal and the bully lets out something that not even you knows [sic]. Bullies usually know something personal about you."

Students also identified through several activities the places where bullying occurs. According to the school maps created by the group members during one session, there was consensus that bullying occurred in hallways, bathrooms, and the cafeteria because there are no adults or few adults in these environments. Students reported that bullying occurred in the school stairwells, as illustrated by the following statement: "All stairwells have people standing in them or someone falls down from a fight." This student reported that bullying occurred in the stairwells because people are standing "... closer together, throwing books, and there's a lot of people on them." Several students reported that bullying occurred in some teachers' classrooms, but not in others.

Acceptability Measures

Group members and group leaders provided feedback relevant to intervention acceptability. Findings are reported separately for the two sources.

Group Member Evaluations. Judging by the consistently positive feedback on the group member evaluation forms, the intervention was strongly accepted by group members. Students were relieved to learn that they were not alone in their experiences and feelings: "My feelings are I like what we're doing because I never know [sic] other people felt the same way I do. I never knew people like *Student*, who's pretty popular would be in here and I like what we're doing." Another student reported that group sessions made her happy because: "I was with other people who have been through the same thing I have."

Group members appeared to be relieved to have the opportunity to share their personal experiences with the group. One group member stated, "It was good to let it out because I keep it inside." Another student commented, "I feel much better to let all might [sic] thoughts outs [sic]." Another student said, "I liked it I discussed a lot of feelings that was [sic] in me."

Finally, students expressed positive feelings regarding the group leaders' interest in reducing the frequency and impact of bullying at the school. One student expressed feeling happy, "That somebody is trying to help people out when there [sic] getting bullied." Another felt "... happy because I feel relieved that we are thinking about ways to stop this. . . because, [he] was tired of being bullied and we are finding ways to stop it." Another student reported being "happy. . . because the teacher or group leader was interested in what we had to say."

Group Leader Evaluations. Although the group leaders were more critical of the group sessions than were the group members, group leader feedback was mostly positive. Based on group leaders' reports, acceptability varied widely across groups and sessions. For example, in response to Session 3 (the introduction of the problem-solving model), the eighth grade group leader and the sixth grade group leaders reported that these activities were appropriate for their groups, as evident from statements indicating that group members "participated fully," and from statements such as, ". . . from the group discussion, it seemed that the students were accepting." However, seventh grade group leaders reported "the problem-solving model may have been a little too elementary for the students and somewhat redundant for this age group." The seventh graders did not appear to accept the session well as was noted in one group leader's reflection: "I think they thought the problem ID activity was a waste of time. They did not appear to understand the purpose, as they all wrote the same answers."

Whereas Session 3 seemed less appropriate for and less accepted by seventh graders, Session 5 (drawing the school maps and identifying high bullying areas) was more accepted by seventh graders than other groups. The seventh grade boys reported that they accepted the session "very much [because] they voted on most problem areas and best solutions to decide. They worked together well." Seventh grade girls also accepted this session's activities "very much, [as] they led more than [the group leaders] did, because they were very engaged in the activities." On the other hand, the sixth grade boys did not accept this session "at all [because] they all wanted to draw people beating each other up." The eighth grade girls needed constant redirection during this session, as they all wanted to quit the activity before the session ended.

The group leaders' perceptions of their own performance varied across sessions and leaders. The majority of the time, the perceived student acceptability and appropriateness of the group session appeared to be related to the group leaders' perceptions of their own performance. The more accepted and appropriate the group session, the more pleased the group leaders were of their own performance.

Quantitative Results

Descriptive statistics for pre- and post-test measures of post-traumatic stress symptoms and internalizing problems, school difficulties, and personal adjustment composites from the BASC-2 revealed some positive change. At pre-test, 37% of the sample exceeded the post-traumatic stress symptoms clinical cutoff score of 38 on the PTSD-RI ($M = 34.74$, $SD = 13.89$), and 33% of the sample exceeded the cut-off at post-test ($M = 30.85$, $SD = 13.54$). However, only 11% of students exceeded the clinical cutoff for internalizing problems at pre-test ($M = 54.48$, $SD = 10.29$), and less than 4% exceed the internalizing problems cutoff at post-test ($M = 53.26$, $SD = 10.21$). For the other BASC-2 composites, the School Problems mean at pre-test was 53.56 ($SD = 12.79$) and at post-test was 54.59 ($SD = 12.70$). The Personal Adjustment mean at pre-test was 48.04 ($SD = 10.63$) and at post-test was 48.78 ($SD = 11.95$). For all constructs, individual variability was relatively stable over time. The pre-post correlations were $r = .83$, $p < .001$ for post-traumatic stress symptoms; $r = .75$, $p < .001$ for internalizing problems; $r = .87$, $p < .001$ for school problems; and $r = .73$, $p < .001$ for personal adjustment.

Repeated measures analyses of variance were used to investigate whether mean levels of the constructs differed from pre- to post-test and whether differences between pre- and post-tests differed by gender. For post-traumatic stress symptoms, the 2 (time) by 2 (gender) ANOVA indicated a statistically significant difference in mean levels between pre-test ($M = 34.64$, $SE = 2.67$) and post-test ($M = 30.80$, $SE = 2.64$), $F(1,25) = 5.96$, $p = .02$, $\eta_p^2 = .19$. This change over time did not vary significantly as a function of gender, $F(1,25) = 0.67$, $p = .69$, $\eta_p^2 = .03$. A 2 (time) by 2 (gender) multivariate ANOVA examined whether students' BASC-2 scores (internalizing problems, school problems and personal adjustment) changed from pre- to post-test. There were no significant multivariate changes, $F(3,23) = 0.59$, $p = .66$, $\eta_p^2 = .09$, nor was there a statistically significant multivariate effect of gender, $F(3,23) = 3.00$, $p = .07$, $\eta_p^2 = .26$.

These findings suggest that middle school students who are identified by school personnel as victims of bullying can experience high levels of post-traumatic stress symptoms even if they do not meet the clinical cutoff for internalizing problems. Further, even though scores on the BASC-2's global measures of problems and adjustment did not change between pre- and post-test, post-traumatic stress symptoms significantly decreased. Since levels of post-traumatic stress symptoms were high at both points of measurement and there was no control group, it is not possible to determine the extent to which the decreased post-traumatic stress symptoms was due to true change associated with the intervention versus regression to the mean.

DISCUSSION

The Peer Victimization Intervention (PVI) illustrates an application of PCSIM as an effective way to develop, implement, and begin to evaluate a culture-specific intervention. Evidence suggests that the application of the initial phases of this model was effective in several ways. Consistent with prior research using this model (e.g., Nastasi et al., 1998, Nastasi et al., 2000; Varjas et al., 2005), this intervention was acceptable to participants and group leaders. Further, there is evidence that involving cultural brokers and stakeholders encouraged acceptability, treatment integrity, and ecological validity.

Evidence of treatment integrity and adaptation of the intervention from group leader journals and interviews indicated that sessions were differentially applicable to diverse groups of students, leading to modifications in implementation and resulting in an intervention targeted specifically to the local population. This view of treatment integrity is congruent with prior research using the PCSIM in which integrity is viewed as reflecting how an intervention is modified to meet local needs while still maintaining the core integrity of the intervention (e.g., Nastasi et al., 2000). This is an important modification as other approaches to treatment integrity seek to determine whether the intervention is implemented in a prescribed manner based on a pre-determined intervention protocol (e.g., Gresham, 1989). In addition, quantitative findings indicated that the culture-specific pilot intervention may have reduced negative mental health stressors related to post-traumatic stress symptoms. These findings support other research using PSCIM as an effective model to develop interventions that have high acceptability and are effective (e.g., Nastasi et al., 2000).

Qualitative data provided information about the causes and consequences of bullying in this specific setting. Race and physical differences as well as perceived sexual orientation, poor hygiene, and being new to the school system were key reasons for being bullied. Bully victims often responded to bullying with ineffective strategies such as aggression or withdrawal and this often occurred because of fear about how they would be perceived. Students identified locations where bullying occurred, including hallways, stairwells, bathrooms, and the cafeteria. Bullying varied across classrooms implying that teachers differ in their use of strategies that minimize bullying. In addition, students were often disappointed with adults' failure to respond to bullying in school. Although these findings replicate extant bullying research (e.g., Espelage & Swearer, 2003; Rodkin & Hodges, 2003), they also provide a robust description of the contexts in which bullying occurred in the particular cultural setting of this middle school.

This article has provided a detailed example of how the PCSIM can be implemented with multiple data collection sources. It also illustrates the importance of recursive collection and analysis of data where early findings influence later data collection until in-depth and focused understandings are obtained. This process was used in the context of mixed methods where ethnographic techniques (e.g., participant observation, key informant and in-depth interviews) were used to gather culturally rich data and quantitative data (e.g., from standardized measures) provided important information about baseline and post-intervention behaviors relevant to post traumatic stress disorder. The qualitative findings about bullying and treatment acceptability help to explain the quantitative results and provide additional support for tentative conclusions that this intervention accounted for observed quantitative pre-post differences.

The combination of methods as well as the active participation of key members of the local school community assisted efforts to address multicultural issues in developing a culture-specific intervention. Researchers/interventionists developed a culture-specific curriculum based on a participatory process of qualitative data collection to inform the session content. In particular, data identified by stakeholders and participants regarding multicultural issues (e.g., ethnicity, sexual orientation) were used to facilitate curriculum development. This supports prior literature indicating that PCSIM can facilitate the development and implementation of culturally valid interventions (e.g., Nastasi et al., 1998; Varjas et al., 2005).

Limitations and Implications

The data collected in application of these early phases of PCSIM have limitations. For example, this was a small sample that included only students who were described by educators as victims of bullying. Also, the pilot intervention did not include a control group. Although later phases of the model would address these issues, it is important to be cautious in reaching conclusions subsequent to these early phases of the model, particularly about the effectiveness of the intervention.

The dual role of researchers as interventionists presents the possibility of researcher bias due to the researchers' investment in the study's findings. In this example, we attempted to reduce bias by: (a) prolonged engagement in the target school, (b) use of cultural brokers, (c) conducting periodic member checks, and (d) involving stakeholders throughout various phases of the PCSIM process (Nastasi et al., 2004). The dual interventionist-researcher role also provides advantages as researchers establish long-term relationships, make important culture-specific modifications to the curriculum, and increase credibility and acceptability of the intervention.

The notion of culture specificity that underlies this work challenges concepts of generalizability. To achieve cultural specificity, each new application of an intervention must be subjected to brokering and formative research to develop unique strategies that have the greatest chance of efficacy in the local setting. A major premise is that the "process" of achieving culture specificity is transferable (generalizable), even though the specific implementation methods and even some findings may not be. It is for this reason that we argue that descriptions of intervention-research process in applied research must include in-depth information about context, participants and procedures related to implementation.

The Peer Victimization Intervention (PVI) provides an example of how a school psychologist can be influential as a researcher-interventionist in developing, implementing, and evaluating a culture-specific intervention. The PCSIM process provides a road map for psychologists to link research with practice so that a maximum number of children profit from their work. It is important to recognize that the process of implementing this model, which involves active input from participants and formative and outcome research, is time consuming and requires intensive effort from competent practitioners. Psychologists could strengthen their efforts to implement this model by working collaboratively with teams of professionals.

ACKNOWLEDGMENT

The authors would like to thank the school system, the stakeholders, and participants who have invested their time and energy into this project. Funding for this work was provided through grants from the Society for the Study of School Psychology (SSSP) and the National Association of School Psychologists (NASP). Additional funding was received from Georgia State University College of Education Educational Research Bureau (Principal Investigators Varjas, Dew, & Meyers).

REFERENCES

Batsche, G. M. & Knoff, H. M. (1994). Bullies and their victims: Understanding a pervasive problem in the schools. *School Psychology Review, 23,* 165-174.

Bronfenbrenner, U. (1989). Ecological systems. *Annals of Child Development, 6,* 187-249.

Cianciotto, J., & Cahill, S. (2003). *Education policy: Issues affecting lesbian, gay, bisexual, and transgender youth.* New York: The National Gay and Lesbian Task Force Policy Institute.

Committee for Children. (1997). *Second Step: A Violence Prevention Curriculum, Middle School/Junior High.* Seattle, WA: Committee for Children.

Dumas, J. E., Rollock, D., Prinz, R. J., Hops, H., & Blechman, E. A. (1999). Cultural sensitivity: Problems and solutions in applied and preventive intervention. *Applied and Preventive Psychology, 8,* 175-196.

Elias, M. J., & Branden, L. R. (1988). Primary prevention of behavioral and emotional problems in school-aged populations. *School Psychology Review, 17,* 581-592.

Espelage, D. L., & Swearer, S. M. (2003). Research on school bullying and victimization: What have we learned and where do we go from here? *School Psychology Review, 32,* 365-383.

Forero, R., McLellan, L., Rissel, C., & Baum, A. (1999). Bullying behaviour and psychosocial health among students in New South Wales, Austraila. *British Medical Journal, 319,* 344-348.

Furlong, M., Morrison, G., & Pavelski, R. (2000). Trends in school psychology for the 21st century: Influences of school violence on professional change. *Psychology in Schools, 37,* 81-90.

Goenjian, A. K., Pynoos, R. S., Steinberg, A. M., Najarian, L. M., Asarnow, J. R., Karayan, I. et al. (1995). Psychiatric comorbidity in children after the 1988 earthquake in Armenia. *Journal of the American Academy of Child and Adolescent Psychiatry, 34,* 1193-1201.

Gresham, F.M. (1989). Assessment of treatment integrity in school consultation and prereferral intervention. *School Psychology Review, 18,* 37-50.

Gutkin, T. B., & Conoley, J. C. (1990). Reconceptualizing school psychology from a service delivery perspective: Implications for practice, training, and research. *Journal of School Psychology, 28,* 203-223.

Ho, B. S. (2002). Application of participatory action research to family-school intervention. *School Psychology Review, 31,* 106-121.

Lazarus, R. S. & Folkman, S. (1984). *Stress, appraisal, and coping.* New York: Springer.

Leff, S. S., Power, T. J., Costigan, T. E., & Manz, P. H. (2003). Assessing the climate of the playground and lunchroom: Implications for bullying prevention programming. *School Psychology Review, 32,* 418-430.

Leff, S. S., Power, T. J., Costigan, T. E., & Nabors, L. A. (2001). School-based aggression prevention programs for young children: Current status and implications for violence prevention. *School Psychology Review, 30,* 343-360.

Lincoln, Y. S., & Guba, E. G. (1985). *Naturalistic inquiry.* Thousands Oaks, CA: Sage.

Nansel, T. R., Overpeck, M., Pilla, R. S., Ruan, W. J., Simons-Morton, B., & Scheidt, P. (2001). Bullying behaviors among U.S. youth: Prevalence and association with psychosocial adjustment. *Journal of the American Medical Association, 285,* 2094-2100.

Nastasi, B. K. (1998). A model for mental health programming in schools and communities. *School Psychology Review, 27,* 165-174.

Nastasi, B. K., & DeZolt, D. M. (1994). *School interventions for children of alcoholics.* NY: Guilford.

Nastasi, B. K., Moore, R. B., & Varjas, K. M. (2004). *School-based mental health services: Creating comprehensive and culturally specific programs.* Washington, DC: American Psychological Association.

Nastasi, B. K., Schensul, J. J., de Silva, M. W. A., Varjas, K., Silva, K. T., Ratnayake, P., & Schensul, S. L. (1998-1999). Community-based sexual risk prevention program for Sri Lankan youth: Influencing sexual-risk decision making. *International Quarterly of Community Health Education, 18,* 139-155.

Nastasi, B. K., Varjas, K., Bernstein, R., & Jayasena, A. (2000). Conducting participatory culture-specific consultation: A global perspective on multicultural consultation. *School Psychology Review, 29,* 401-413.

Nastasi, B. K., Varjas, K., Jayasena, A., Bernstein Moore, R., Sarkar, S., Hitchcock, J., & Burkholder, G. (2005). *Sri Lanka mental health promotion project.* Unpublished manuscript. Minneapolis, MN: Walden University School of Psychology.

Nastasi, B. K., Varjas, K., Sarkar, S., & Jayasena, A. (1998). Participatory model of mental health programming: Lessons learned from work in a developing country. *School Psychology Review, 27* (2), 217-232.

Nastasi, B. K., Varjas, K., Schensul, J. J., Schensul, S. L., Silva, K. T., & Ratnayake, P. (2000). The participatory intervention model: A framework for conceptualizing and promoting intervention acceptability. *School Psychology Quarterly, 15,* 207-232.

Olweus, D. (1993). *Bullying at school: What we know and what we can do.* Oxford: Blackwell.

Pellegrini, A. D., Bartini, M., & Brooks, F. (1999). School bullies, victims, and aggressive victims: Factors relating to the group affiliation and victimization in early adolescence. *Journal of Educational Psychology, 91,* 216-224.

Pynoos, R. S., Goenjian, A., Tashjian, M., Karakashian, M., Manjikian, R., Manoukian, G., Steinberg, A. M., & Fairbanks, L. A. (1993). Post-traumatic stress reactions in children after the 1988 Armenian earthquake. *British Journal of Psychiatry, 63,* 239-247.

Reynolds, C. R. & Kamphaus, R. (2004). *The Behavior Assessment Scale for Children: Second Edition.* Circle Pines, MN: AGS Publishing Inc.

Rivers, I. (2001). The bullying of sexual minorities at school: Its nature and long-term correlates. *Educational and Child Psychology, 18,* 32-46.

Rodkin, P. C., & Hodges, E. V. E. (2003). Bullies and victims in the peer ecology: Four questions for psychologists and school professionals. *School Psychology Review, 32,* 384-400.

Roland, E. (2002). Bullying, depressive symptoms and suicidal thoughts. *Educational Research, 44,* 55-67.

Roussos, A., Goenjian, A. K., Steinberg, A. M., Sotiropoulou, C., Kakaki, M., Kabakos, C. et al. (2005). Posttraumatic stress and depressive reactions among children and adolescents after the 1999 earthquake in Ano Liosia, Greece. *American Journal of Psychiatry, 162,* 530-537.

Salmon, G., James, A., Cassidy, E. L., & Javaloyes, M. A. (2000). Bullying a review: Presentations to an adolescent psychiatric services and within a school for emotionally and behaviourally disturbed children. *Clinical Child Psychology and Psychiatry, 5,* 563-579.

Salmon, G., James, A., & Smith, D. M. (1998). Bullying in schools: Self reported anxiety, depression, and self esteem in secondary children. *British Medical Journal, 317,* 924-925.

Sheridan, S. M., & Gutkin, T. B. (2000). The ecology of school psychology: Examining and changing our paradigm for the 21st century. *School Psychology Review, 29,* 485-502.

Slee, P. T. (1994). Situational and interpersonal correlates of anxiety associated with peer victimization. *Child Psychiatry and Human Development, 25,* 97-107.

Snyder, J., Brooker, M., Patrick, M. R., Snyder, A., Schrepferman, L., & Stoolmiller, M. (2003). Observed peer victimization during early elementary school: Continuity, growth, and relation to risk for child antisocial and depressive behavior. *Child Development, 74,* 1881-1898.

Stockdale, M. S., Hangaduamdo, S., Duys, D., Larson, K., & Sarvela, P. D. (2002). Rural elementary students', parents', and teachers' perceptions of bullying. *American Journal of Health Behavior, 29,* 239-268.

Varjas, K., Nastasi, B. K., Moore, R. B., & Jayasena, A. (2005). Using ethnographic methods for development of culture-specific interventions. *Journal of School Psychology, 43,* 241-258.

Wolke, D., Woods, S., Bloomfield, L., & Karstadt, L. (2001). Bullying involvement in primary school and common health problems. *Archives of Disease in Childhood, 85,* 197-201.

doi:10.1300/J370v22n02_03

Targeting English Language Learners, Tasks, and Treatments in Instructional Consultation

Emilia C. Lopez

Queens College, City University of New York

SUMMARY. English language learners (ELL) are typically instructed in general education programs that do not have bilingual instructional support (Zehler et al., 2003). Teachers instructing those students must focus on strengthening the students' English language skills because language is such a primary component for learning and achieving. Instructional consultation is a service delivery model that provides classroom teachers with the support they need to implement effective instructional practices to increase ELL students' language proficiency skills in English. However, the implications are that instructional consultants and consultees working with this population must approach the consultation process while addressing second language acquisition issues. Instructional consultation focuses on exploring the interaction between the learner, the task and the treatment. This article explores those three components when providing instructional consultation to target ELLs' language instructional needs in non-bilingual settings. doi:10.1300/J370v22n02_04 *[Article copies available for a fee from The Haworth Document Delivery Service: 1-800-HAWORTH. E-mail address: <docdelivery@haworthpress.com> Website: <http://www.HaworthPress.com> © 2006 by The Haworth Press, Inc. All rights reserved.]*

Address correspondence to: Emilia C. Lopez, PhD, Queens College-City University of New York, Department of Educational and Community Programs, 65-30 Kissena Boulevard, Flushing, NY 11367 (E-mail: lopez@cedx.com).

[Haworth co-indexing entry note]: "Targeting English Language Learners, Tasks, and Treatments in Instructional Consultation." Lopez, Emilia C. Co-published simultaneously in *Journal of Applied School Psychology* (The Haworth Press, Inc.) Vol. 22, No. 2, 2006, pp. 59-79; and: *Multicultural Issues in School Psychology* (ed: Bonnie K. Nastasi) The Haworth Press, Inc., 2006, pp. 59-79. Single or multiple copies of this article are available for a fee from The Haworth Document Delivery Service [1-800-HAWORTH, 9:00 a.m. - 5:00 p.m. (EST). E-mail address: docdelivery@haworthpress.com].

KEYWORDS. English as a second language, consultation, instructional methods, school psychology roles

English language learners (ELLs)[1] are in the process of acquiring English as a second language and demonstrate limitations in their abilities to speak, read, and/or write in English (de Valenzuela & Niccolai, 2004). Recent statistics for public schools estimate that (a) between 2002 and 2003 approximately 4 million students were identified as ELL in grades K through 12; (b) those students represent 8% of the total public school population; (c) ELL students are represented in approximately 400 languages; and (d) the languages most frequently spoken by ELL students are Spanish, Vietnamese, Hmong, Haitian Creole, Cantonese, and Korean (National Center for Education Statistics [NCES)], 2005; National Clearinghouse for English Language Acquisition and Language Instruction, 2001).

Bilingual education programs are available for ELL students that provide instruction in English and the students' native language. However, the majority of ELL students do not have access to bilingual education programs and the number of ELL students who receive services in their native language has significantly decreased between 1992 and 2002 (National Clearinghouse for English Language Acquisition and Language Instruction, 2001; Zehler et al., 2003).

A lack of funding for bilingual education programs and a shortage of qualified bilingual personnel to instruct students in a variety of languages other than English has contributed to limited access to bilingual education programs. Zheler et al. (2003) report that ELL students are typically instructed in non-bilingual classroom settings while receiving support services via English as a second language (ESL)[2] programs. ESL services are "a system of instruction that enables students who are not proficient in English . . . to acquire academic proficiency in spoken and written English" (Ovando, Collier & Combs, 2003, p. 6). ESL services are most frequently provided on a pull-out basis (Zheler et al., 2003). ESL services also include specialized ESL sheltered instruction programs that use ESL methodology to teach language as well as content knowledge (e.g., Science, Social Studies) in English for part of the school day (Ovando et al.). Some districts report not having any ESL services available and instead provide support to ELL students through classroom aides, Title 1 or other resource teachers, tutors, or special education personnel (Zehler et al.).

ELL students with disabilities are typically instructed in non-bilingual classroom settings. ELL students with disabilities represent 9% of all ELL students in public schools; 75% of districts educating those students report a lack of specialized services such as bilingual special education programs or bilingual resource rooms (Zehler et al., 2003). For the most part, schools provide support to ELL students with disabilities by offering both ESL and special education services, or by tapping the knowledge base of staff in those two programs and in bilingual education programs to integrate instructional support services.

Ovando et al. (2003) point out that the majority of teachers who educate ELL students, in general or special education programs, report receiving little training to instruct this student population. NCES data for the 1999-2000 school year indicate that 41% of teachers in public schools taught ELL students; yet only 12.5% of those teachers had 8 or more hours of training on how to instruct that population (NCES, 2002). The problem is compounded in school districts that have little or no ESL support because classroom teachers who lack ESL training are still expected to instruct ELL students with little or no instructional support (Ovando et al., 2003).

A lack of bilingual and ESL programs and a shortage of teachers who are well trained to instruct ELL students are accompanied by concerns regarding the achievement of ELL students. In a study designed to examine the services provided to ELL students, the findings indicated that 76% of third grade ELL students were below grade level in reading and approximately 53% of eighth graders in this population were below grade level in mathematics (Zehler et al., 2003). Statistics indicating below grade level functioning for ELL students are accompanied by concerns that significant numbers of culturally and linguistically diverse students, including ELL students, are not achieving as well as non-minority students and have a higher prevalence of suspensions, grade retentions, expulsions, drop out rates, and referrals to special education (Meece & Kurtz-Costes, 2001). These findings speak to the challenges that educators confront in reaching the goal of helping these students to achieve academic success.

Educators and school psychologists have made multiple recommendations to address the instructional needs of ELL students that include: (a) providing teachers with training to instruct ELL students; (b) providing funding for bilingual and ESL programs; (c) establishing co-teaching partnerships between bilingual, ESL, special education, and general education teachers; and (d) creating prevention programs that provide support to ELL students within general education (Chamot, 1998;

Gersten & Jimenez, 1998; Ovando et al., 2003). Instructional consultation (IC) is recommended as a preventative delivery model designed to provide support to teachers of ELL students (Lopez & Truesdell, in press). Since most ELL students are instructed in non-bilingual settings and teachers have little training as to how to instruct this population, the emphasis of this article is on exploring the implications of using IC to support teacher consultees instructing ELL students in non-bilingual classroom settings. The subsequent sections of this article also emphasize language and second language acquisition. For ELL students, issues of language development and second language acquisition take the forefront because, according to Ovando et al. (2003), "Language is usually the most salient issue as language minority students establish their role within the classroom. It is the dominant theme in the instructional process" (p. 22).

INSTRUCTIONAL CONSULTATION FOR ELL STUDENTS

Various consultation models (e.g., mental health, behavioral, organizational) are available that share similar processes in terms of stages (i.e., contracting, problem identification, problem analysis, intervention planning and delivery, process and outcome evaluation), and foci (i.e., collaboration, problem solving, and indirect service delivery) (Brown, Pryzwansky, & Schulte, 2001). The IC model is unique because of its emphasis on integrating consultation research and practice with knowledge of instructional psychology and interventions (Rosenfield, 1987). Instructional consultants collaborate with teachers to identify students' strengths and deficits with respect to prior knowledge and other alterable variables; examine the instructional environment (e.g., curriculum, assignments); and plan, implement, and evaluate instructional interventions.

Research investigating the impact of IC suggests that the model is effective in terms of preventing minority students' instructional problems (Gravois & Rosenfield, 2006; Silva & Rosenfield, 2004). Silva (2005) conducted an investigation to explore special education referral and placement outcomes for ELLs. The data indicated that instructional consultation teams (ICTs) were found to be more effective than prereferral interventions teams in decreasing special education referrals and placements for ELL students. The results also suggested that ICTs lowered special education referrals more for non-ELL students than for ELL students and that ELL students were ultimately more likely than non-ELL students to be referred and classified as handicapped (Silva & Rosenfield, 2004). Based on the results of the investigation, Silva and Rosenfield recommend "developing IC Teams training modules targeted at meeting the needs of ELL students, training IC Teams members on second language acquisition, [and] performing native language curriculum-based assessment. . . " (Implications section, ¶ 3).

The results of the investigation conducted by Silva (2005) imply that IC has the potential to address ELL students' instructional needs. Rosenfield (1987) argues that IC

> . . . forces us to shift the focus from the defective learner to viewing the learner as part of an instructional system. The major components of the system include three sets of variables: the task or what is to be learned; the learner, in terms of his or her academic readiness to undertake the learning task; and the treatment, or the instructional and management strategies. (p. 10)

Focusing on the instruction system is pivotal when working with ELL students to avoid the assumption that those students' perceived difficulties in learning English and in achieving in reading and content areas such as Science and Math are due to learning problems inherent to the students. The shift in this approach comes from examining the ELL student, not in isolation and as a "deficient" learner, but as a learner who is demonstrating expected developmental transitions within the second language acquisition process, or as a learner who may be demonstrating difficulties because of problems inherent to the instructional system (e.g., a poor match between the instructional components and the students' knowledge and/or skills). However, the status of the learner as ELL means that instructional consultants must examine the (a) learner, (b) task, and (c) instructional environment with particular attention to language development and second language acquisition issues. Within group differences also should be considered to avoid stereotyping (e.g., assuming that all students within a language group have similar characteristics) and to account for the individual characteristics of each learner.

Focus on the English Language Learner

Within the context of the learner, Rosenfield (1987) refers to exploring the student's readiness to undertake the learning task and succeed in the classroom environment. Since ELL students are still in the process of acquiring English as a second language, much of their readiness to succeed in classroom tasks is related to their level of English language proficiency. Instructional consultants can explore several issues with consultees about their ELL students' English language skills that include social and academic language skills, variables impacting the second language acquisition process, and expected developmental processes within the stages of second language acquisition.

The learners' social and academic language skills. Cummins (1984) developed the concepts of Basic Interpersonal Communicative Skills (BICS) in comparison to Cognitive Academic Language Proficiency Skills (CALPS). He defined BICS as "the manifestation of language proficiency in everyday communicative contexts" and CALPS as "the manipulation of language in decontextualized academic situations" (p. 137). The available research in second language acquisition indicates that second language learners tend to acquire BICS in two to three years (Cummins, 1984). Within that amount of time, most students are able to develop adequate vocabulary, syntax and comprehension skills to be able to use the second language in situations such as discussing what they did during the weekend, or their comprehension of familiar reading material that is supported by contexts such as pictures, concrete stimuli, and everyday experiences. However, the research also indicates that it generally takes between 5 to 10 years for students to master a second language in academic situations in which the language is more de-contextualized (e.g., language is more abstract and not supported by contextual cues such as visual stimuli) (Collier, 1992; Cummins, 1986). Instructional consultants will find it useful to engage consultees in considering the social and academic language skills those students are bringing into each instructional situation and how those levels of skills impact the students' ability to approach instructional tasks.

Variables impacting the learner's second language acquisition skills. Research suggests that students who have well-developed academic language skills in their first language are able to gain CALPS in English at a faster rate because high proficiency in the first language facilitates the transfer of knowledge to the second language (Cummins & Swain, 1986). Cummins refers to this phenomenon as the common underlying proficiency theory. For example, if students understand and can explain the concept of "community" in the first language, they will be able to understand and discuss that concept in the second language once they acquire the vocabulary, syntax and language fluency in that second language. The empirical literature indicates that common underlying proficiency leads to positive gains in reading, writing, and vocabulary skills in English (Ellis, 1994; Ordoñez, Carlo, Snow, & McLaughlin, 2002; Ovando et al., 2003).

A second student factor that strongly influences second language acquisition is the students' past educational history. Students with little or no prior access to educational experiences demonstrate more difficulties not only in second language acquisition but also in their ability to succeed in academic tasks (Baca & Cervantes, 2004). The type of support that the students received in earlier grades is also important. For example, ELL students who are not provided with ESL support, who receive ESL support inconsistently, or who do not receive ESL support in content areas struggle with language proficiency as well as with their academic subjects (Gersten, Marks, Keating, & Baker, 1998).

Expected developmental processes within the stages of second language acquisition. Krashen (1982) refers to five stages of language acquisition: (a) Level 1: Pre-Production (i.e., learners demonstrate little or no comprehension and limited or no verbal production in the second language), (b) Level 2: Early Production (i.e., learners demonstrate poor comprehension, and verbal production is limited to isolated words or two word utterances), (c) Level 3: Speech Emergence (i.e., learners demonstrate adequate comprehension and use short phrases and simple sentences; errors are common), (d) Level 4: Intermediate Fluency (i.e., learners demonstrate well developed comprehension and adequate expressive skills), and (e) Level 5: Advanced Fluency (i.e., learners demonstrate excellent receptive and expressive language skills).[3] In general, an understanding of the stages of second language acquisition will help consultees to establish a connection between the learners' English language skills and their readiness to succeed in instructional tasks. Instructional consultants also examine the students' functioning within expected second language acquisition processes such as the silent period (i.e., developmental stage in the early stages of second language acquisition in which students typically do not produce in the second language and are instead attuned to receptive aspects of the second language), language loss (i.e., common experience of bilinguals in which language loss is experienced in the first language as a result of using the second language more frequently and gaining more proficiency in the second language), and code switching (i.e., entails bilinguals using both languages within one sentence to communicate as in "Come on, vamonos.") (Ovando et al., 2003).

Focus on the Tasks

Instructional consultation focusing on students' tasks means examining "what is to be learned" or the characteristics of the task (Rosenfield, 1987, p. 10). Within the context of second language acquisition, instructional consultants explore the characteristics of the tasks in relationship to the skills required by the task and the students' perceptions of the task.

Skills required by the task. Part of examining the task in IC entails exploring the skills that the task requires and the match between those required skills and the students' ability. As such, instructional consultants and consultees must be particularly attentive to the prior knowledge or skills that classroom tasks require from the students. For example, Math or Science tasks that require specific prior knowledge may be difficult for students with little or no previous educational backgrounds or for immigrant ELL students who were previously educated in countries with distinct curricula and teaching methods. Tasks also may call for culturally distinct knowledge that immigrant ELL students may lack.

Instructional consultants also should explore how comprehensible the tasks are for ELL students. Krashen (1982) refers to comprehensible input and defines it as language provided to students that is at the learners' level and slightly above that level to provide a margin of challenge. It is similar to the concept of providing students with tasks that are at their instructional level so that the content is manageable with some instructional support (Rosenfield, 1987). Instructional tasks that are not comprehensible have vocabulary and language structures (e.g., syntax, grammar) that are at the students' frustration level whereas tasks that have comprehensible input match the students' levels of language proficiency in the areas of speaking, listening, reading and writing. The questions provided in Table 1 are useful to instructional consultants as they explore the language skills required by different instructional tasks with consultees.

The learners' perceptions of the task. The students' perceptions of the tasks are additional components to consider in the IC process (Baca & Cervantes, 2004). Culturally different students who are recent immigrants bring to classroom situations their own attitudes about learning and instructional tasks that are based on their previous schooling experiences. Students from regions such as Latin America and Asia, for example, were typically taught in their native lands using traditional instructional settings that emphasized rote learning, teacher led instructional sequences, and conventional tests (e.g., tests where they have to

TABLE 1. Questions Relevant to Language Skills Required by Instructional Tasks

---

1. Are the task's oral and/or written directions comprehensible to the student?
2. What is the level of vocabulary, grammar, and syntax of the task and how do those relate to the student's levels of language proficiency?
3. What levels of social and academic language proficiency does the task require?
4. Do the instructions for the task have multiple steps and does the student understand each of those steps?
5. Are resource materials and tasks (i.e., internet resources, textbooks, reference books, additional readings, handouts) at the student's appropriate instructional and language proficiency levels?
6. Are response modes for the task (e.g., student can provide response via oral or written responses) adapted to the student's level of language proficiency and competencies?
7. What are the goals of the task and are tasks provided in which students can demonstrate a variety of skills (e.g., content knowledge vs. language competence in writing)?
8. What prior knowledge or experiences do the tasks require (e.g., prior knowledge in math or prior life experiences)?
9. Are tasks accompanied by tools such as concrete stimuli, models, and pictures to provide ELL students with contextual support?
10. Are tasks accompanied by modeling, demonstrations, and experiential activities that provide ELL students with contextual support?
11. Are multicultural tasks and materials used that are of interest to the ELL students in the classroom?

---

show memorization of content) (Ovando et al., 2003). For these students, encountering unfamiliar instructional strategies such as discovery learning tasks (i.e., students are provided guidance from the teacher and support materials to engage in independent tasks that lead to "discovering" concepts, facts, and relationships) and cooperative learning activities (i.e., students work in group settings) sometimes leads them to question the value and purposes of such experiences as genuine learning tools (Lopez, Liu, Popoutsakis, Rafferty, & Valero, 1998; Ovando et al., 2003). In middle and high school settings, for example, having discussions with immigrant ELL students is helpful to explore the concept of diversity in the ways that we teach, learn and show knowledge (Lopez et al., 1998).

Focus on the Treatment

Rosenfield (1987) defines the treatment as "the instructional and management strategies" used to teach instructional tasks (p. 10). Currently, there is insufficient research available to clearly guide instructional consultants and teacher consultees as to what are effective practices in instructing ELL students. However, there is an available knowledge base that can guide instructional consultants and teacher consultees. Given the focus of the manuscript on second language acquisition issues, a discussion follows related to (a) quality language instruction for English language learners and (b) ESL instructional practices.[4]

Quality instruction for ELL students. In an effort to synthesize the available knowledge about this topic, Gersten and Baker (2000) used a multivocal synthesis method to integrate three sets of data sources. The researchers looked at quantitative intervention investigations that used experimental or quasi-experimental designs as well as "descriptive studies of instructional practices that utilized classroom observation techniques" (p. 33). In addition, they included professional work groups with practitioners (i.e., teachers, administrators and researchers) to "tap into participants' concepts about effective instructional practices for English-language learners" (p. 37). A meta-analysis of the quantitative investigations found that the studies with the largest overall effect sizes used interventions that were introduced and validated by instructional pioneers such as Brophy and Good (1986). Among those intervention strategies were pre-teaching key vocabulary that is connected to instructional content; providing students with feedback about their use of English to communicate effectively; teaching problem solving and comprehension of math word problems; building student background knowledge; and increasing academic engagement. The qualitative studies suggested that effective instructional programs emphasized small-group and individual instructional groupings. The professional work groups concluded that classrooms with ELL students needed to emphasize frequent and extended student responses, modeling, think-alouds, and academic talk or discussions of instructional concepts. The work groups also recommended a series of strategies to integrate the teaching of English language skills with content learning such as emphasizing oral, written and academic language; using visuals and written language to teach verbal content in English; and focusing on fewer vocabulary words per lesson but enhancing the breadth and depth of the vocabulary words covered.

Gersten and Baker (2000) also identified a total of five instructional principles that have "limited experimental evidence" (p. 62) but are critical elements for instruction. The first principle involves teaching vocabulary throughout the curriculum. The teachers in the work groups recommended choosing vocabulary words that are (a) useful in conveying key concepts within the curriculum, (b) frequently used in the lessons or tasks, (c) related to the content being taught, and (d) relevant to the students (i.e., choose words that are meaningful in terms of students' interests and experiences). The second principle recommended was the use of story maps and other visual strategies (e.g., pictures, words written on the board, graphic organizers, concept maps, word banks, writing key words on flip charts) to teach concepts and vocabulary. The third recommendation entailed the use of cooperative learning and peer tutoring strategies to teach ELL students reading, reading comprehension and content knowledge. The fourth intervention is a controversial and difficult strategy that involves the "strategic" use of the native language in helping students to develop content knowledge and high order thinking skills. The intervention was described as strategic because it requires teacher judgment to decide when students need content or tasks provided in the native language to explain complex concepts. In essence, the utility of the strategy lies in helping ELL students to capture knowledge in the native language instead of relying on their limited English skills and perhaps missing key content or concepts. The researchers cautioned that there is research suggesting that constant translation is not an effective technique because students then rely on the knowledge that the material will be repeated in their native language and "tune out" content in English. The fifth strategy involves modulating the relationship between the level of difficulty of a concept and the language used to discuss the content. Gersten and Baker elaborate:

> Typically, there is an invert relationship between the two [cognitive and language demands]. When cognitive demands are high, language expectations are simplified, and teachers, for example, may accept brief or truncated responses in English. In another part of the lesson, cognitive demands are intentionally reduced so that students can more comfortably experiment with extended English-language use. (pp. 65-66)

Also available are empirical investigations suggesting that ELLs benefit from reading instruction in decoding and phonology skills. Leafstedt, Richards and Gerber (2004) implemented a 10-week intervention program designed to improve the phonological and decoding skills of ELL Kindergarteners. The investigators found that the phonological awareness intervention was more effective than the general kindergarten reading instruction in increasing the students' word reading skills. Similar results were obtained in several studies that used tutoring programs to teach ELL students decoding and phonics skills in English (Denton, Anthony, Parker & Hasbrouck, 2004; Gunn, Biglan, Smolkowsky, & Ary, 2000; Gunn, Smolkowsky, Biglan, & Black, 2002).

Recommended ESL instructional practices. According to Gersten et al. (1998), the ESL curriculum needs to be closely aligned with the classroom curriculum so that the learning that occurs in the ESL setting is meaningful. Collaboration between the classroom and ESL teachers is beneficial in integrating topics, introducing vocabulary, and coordinating multiple learning tasks (e.g., the classroom teacher concentrates on helping the ELL student to draft a book report and the ESL teacher works with the student on revising and improving a final draft). However, a common barrier is that ESL teachers are often itinerant teachers who travel from school to school and are not closely connected with the classroom curriculum and/or with the students' progress within the curriculum. Borden (1998) also adds that classroom teachers often view ESL as a "place" where students go to learn English and do not recognize the value of integrating the general instructional program with the ESL curriculum. It is thus imperative to not only align the ESL and general education curricula but also to provide opportunities for those teachers to work together to plan for instruction.

ESL programs vary in terms of their teaching approaches and methodologies (Ovando et al., 2003). ESL teachers may use traditional methodologies that are based on psycholinguistic theory (e.g., Grammar-Translation method, Audiolingual Method) and emphasize repetition, memorization, drills, and the presentation of carefully sequenced grammatical structures to teach grammar and syntax. The research suggests that those approaches tend to de-emphasize meaning (e.g., using language in meaningful contexts) and communication in natural situations. Today ESL training programs tend to prepare teachers to use Krashen's (1982) Natural Approach. In this approach the foci are on providing students with language that is comprehensible, creating supportive and low-anxiety classroom settings, allowing learners to make errors, encouraging but not demanding language production until the learner is ready, using language in natural communication situations to promote communicative competence, emphasizing language content rather than form, using whole language approaches to encourage reading and writing in English, and teaching language via meaningful content (Ovando et al., 1998).

PROBLEM IDENTIFICATION
IN INSTRUCTIONAL CONSULTATION

Assessment of ELL students within instructional consultation requires knowledge of second language acquisition, bilingualism, and language proficiency (Rhodes, Ochoa & Ortiz, 2005). Examining the instructional system also mandates the use of a variety of assessment tools to identify the source of the instructional difficulties (i.e., learner, task, treatment). Given the pivotal role of language proficiency in ELL students' learning experiences, assessment of academic learning is enriched by language proficiency data to determine how the student is functioning in terms of academic language skills (CALPS) and within the sequence of the second language acquisition stages.

Several tools are useful for collecting information about ELL students' language proficiency skills in the areas of speaking, listening, reading and writing. Informal language samples collected in either structured (e.g.., teacher introduces a topic and questions about the content or concept) or unstructured (e.g., language sample is collected during an informal classroom discussion) situations (Gottlieb & Hamayan, in press) are most ecologically valid because the language samples are directly connected to the classroom activities and tasks. Checklists or scales are helpful to obtain language proficiency data based on language samples and teacher interviews. The Oral Language Proficiency Rating Scale (Illinois State Board of Education, 1999), for example, is used to rate students' functioning in the areas of grammar, vocabulary, fluency and comprehension. Each of those areas is rated along a 6-point scale (e.g., for vocabulary, the scale ranges from 1 ["Vocabulary limitations are so extreme as to make conversation virtually impossible"] to 6 ["Vocabulary is as accurate and extensive as that of a native speaker of the same age"]).

English language learners are typically given language proficiency tests to determine their level of functioning in English. Several tools are available such as the Woodcock Muñoz Language Survey Revised (WMLS-R; Woodcock & Muñoz-Sandoval, 2005a) and the Woodcock Muñoz Language Proficiency Battery (WMLPB-R; Woodcock & Muñoz-Sandoval, 2005b). Language proficiency tools also provide information about levels of functioning in specific areas. For example, the WMLS-R provides language proficiency levels for oral language, reading, and written language. The WMLPB-R provides assessors with CALP levels that range from Level 1: Negligible to Level 5: Advanced. Although the utility of such language proficiency tools is limited because of their distance from the actual classroom content, the assessment data provide valuable information to share with the consultee about the student's readiness to learn tasks from a language proficiency perspective.

A series of interviews with parents, teachers and other school personnel, such as ESL teachers, is useful in obtaining additional information not only about the student's language skills but also about past educational experiences (Rhodes et al., 2005). Although initially the consultee may present the "problem" as inherent in the ELL student, both interviews and observation methods may be used to examine the instructional environment and the strategies being implemented to teach those students. The questions provided in Table 1, for example, will guide instructional consultants and teacher consultees in examining the relationship between the students' language proficiency skills and the task demands. The discussion provided in the treatment section of this article also may help instructional consultants to explore the types of instructional strategies that the teacher consultees are using within the curriculum.

Systematic observations of instructional environments add valuable data to the IC process (Martines & Rodriquez-Srednicki, in press). Waxman, Tharp, and Soleste Hilberg (2004) provide a comprehensive coverage of various observation tools that have been validated with minority students. For example, the purpose of the Sheltered Instruction Observation Protocol (SIOP) is to collect observation data about instructional issues in sheltered ESL programs (Echevarria & Short, 2004). The Classroom Observation Schedule (COS) also has been used in multiethnic settings to collect data about students' interactions with teachers, classroom activities and materials, and the languages used in the classroom (Waxman & Padron, 2004).

Reading inventories are used to identify the instructional, frustration, and independent levels for instructional tasks such as reading passages (Rosenfield, 1987). Task analyses are particularly helpful in determining the prerequisite language skills and background knowledge that ELL students need to succeed in language arts tasks as well as in content matter tasks. Curriculum based measures (CBM) also have been recommended to assess bilingual students' academic skills (Baker & Good, 1995; McCloskey & Athanasiou, 2000).

Although much information can be gained from assessing the students' academic learning in English, Curriculum-Based Assessment (CBA) conducted bilingually is extremely valuable. For example, assessing how much background knowledge the student has in the native language will clarify if difficulties with concept formation in English are due to limited proficiency in English or to a lack of background knowledge. That strategy also is helpful in determining how much the student benefits from the "strategic" use of the native language (Gersten & Baker, 2000). A bilingual instructional consultant also can work with a teacher consultee to establish if some of the writing, reading and oral errors being made by the student are a function of language interference (i.e., the student is using syntax rules from the native language to produce sentences in English) and to establish interventions to help the student to identify the errors.

PROCESS ISSUES

Thus far the article has focused on instructional consultation by addressing academic learning from the perspective of the learner, task and the treatment. Instructional consultants also must emphasize the process of working with teacher consultees instructing ELL students. Because ELL students often demonstrate deficits in their language skills, consultants and teacher consultees may approach the consultation referral emphasizing the student's language problems and academic difficulties. The consultants' and consultees' cultural biases may interfere with the IC process. Instructional consultants and consultees need to approach the problem identification stage with careful consideration as to how the academic problems are being viewed (Ingraham, 2000). Goldstein and Harris (2000) found barriers in problem identification in two schools where parents and teachers disagreed as to how to instruct bilingual students with special education needs. In those schools conflicting views of students' problems and ways to approach those problems interfered with the consultation process as consultants and consultees could not agree on the implementation of interventions designed to target students' academic needs.

In consultation, part of the challenge may be helping consultees to gain additional knowledge and skills to instruct ELL students. However, perhaps the most formidable challenge is to help the consultee to experience conceptual change (Hylander, 2003). Conceptual changes entail helping the consultee to re-conceptualize the ELL students' academic needs not just within the framework of the students' language deficits but also within the framework of the instructional changes and adaptations that are necessary to help those students succeed academically. As such, a consultee who may initially view an ELL student as unable to solve word problems in mathematics because of perceived memory deficits may change his/her frame of reference when learning that the student can conceptually understand the problem if key vocabulary found in the word problem is taught and learned.

Working with teacher consultees to plan and deliver interventions for ELL students also is approached with consideration of how consultees and clients view the intervention and if they find it acceptable within their cultural contexts (Ingraham, 2000). Meyer's (2002) qualitative investigation of an organizational consultation case focused on school reforms for African America students revealed low treatment acceptability. Pedagogical dissonance, defined by Meyer as dissonance in how consultants and consultees viewed curriculum models for African American students (i.e., consultants emphasized direct instruction and the schools they consulted with emphasized whole language approaches), resulted in consultees rejecting the consultants' instructional methodologies. Meyer concluded that consultants must approach the planning and implementation of interventions with flexibility in responding to consultees' belief systems about instruction and curriculum.

Instructional consultants may easily assume that teacher consultees are not willing to implement recommended interventions because of a lack of sensitivity to cultural or linguistic issues. However, consultants are forewarned not to make such quick assumptions because treatment acceptability and fidelity are related to many different factors for teachers of ELL students (Brown et al., 2001; Lopez et al., 1998). Adapting curriculum for ELL students is challenging, particularly when consultees' classrooms may have multiple ELL students with varied levels of language proficiency and educational and cultural backgrounds. Implementing new strategies to accommodate ELL students may demand new skills, more planning time, and additional resources that discourage teacher consultees from implementing specific interventions as planned (Brown et al.). In those cases the source of the resistance is not related to the teacher's lack of cultural sensitivity but to other generic treatment acceptability and fidelity factors that must be addressed in order to support teacher consultees. Among the supports that teachers of ELL students may need, especially in non-bilingual settings, are background materials or information, observations of other teachers using similar strategies, modeling, coaching, and intervention scripts. Collaborative efforts such as co-teaching with ESL personnel also may be beneficial along with peer collaborative efforts in the form of curriculum planning, organization of activities, and the development of instructional materials.

FUTURE DIRECTIONS
IN RESEARCH, TRAINING, AND PRACTICE

At this point, there is little research focusing on effective instructional strategies for ELL students. There is even less research investigating the process of instructional consultation with ELL students. Investigations are needed to explore effective instructional strategies for ELL students. Evidenced based interventions will help instructional consultants and teacher consultees to identify those interventions that are most likely to increase language and academic skills for ELL students. Studies investigating cultural differences in learning will continue to shed light on our understanding of the complex relationship between culture, learners, instructional tasks and instructional interventions. Cultural differences in communication, interpersonal interactions, and instructional experiences will enhance our knowledge of how to instruct culturally diverse learners and how to manage classrooms using culturally sensitive approaches.

The process of addressing instructional consultation with teacher consultees who instruct ELL students needs to be investigated in order to more clearly understand how to collaborate to implement effective instructional strategies for these students. Ingraham's (2000) multicultural consultation framework provides a road map as to various areas that need further investigation such as cross-cultural communication and collaboration, effective multicultural problem solving strategies, and cultural differences in how problems are viewed.

Identifying problems within instructional consultation will continue to pose a challenge for instructional consultants. The process of assessing the academic skills of ELL students will be enhanced by research investigations that establish the validity of a variety of CBA procedures with this student population. Classroom observation systems are needed to guide instructional consultants in observing cultural and linguistical variables relevant to learners, tasks and treatments.

Training instructional consultants to address the learning needs of ELL students will be facilitated by research based training modules and strategies. Developing research based strategies to train students in practica and internship situations will further enhance trainers' abilities to prepare instructional consultants to address the needs of ELL students in practical settings.

A variety of research methodologies that include quantitative, experimental, quasi-experimental as well as qualitative approaches are needed. Gersten and Baker's (2000) multivocal design is an excellent example of how quantitative and qualitative methods are integrated to further our knowledge base about effective instructional strategies for ELL students.

CONCLUDING REMARKS

The focus of this manuscript has been on exploring the utility of the IC process to provide support services to teachers instructing ELL students outside of bilingual programs. The manuscript also emphasized second language acquisition and proficiency issues. Space limitations did not allow for a comprehensive coverage of other important variables. For example, the article did not cover issues related to culturally sensitive classroom management interventions, which is an important component of IC. Issues related to acculturation and cross-cultural differences in communicative styles were not covered. The research relevant to bilingual instruction was not reviewed. As such, much is yet to be discussed about multicultural issues relevant to IC. Part of the challenge that awaits us is to integrate some of the existing research and knowledge bases from the fields of bilingualism, cross-cultural psychology, bilingual education, ESL methodology, and bilingual special education into our understanding of instructional issues relevant to ELL students. Integrating those various perspectives and approaches will further enrich our ability to understand and implement IC services that are responsive to the needs of this population.

NOTES

1. The terms ELL and limited English proficient (LEP) students are used interchangeably in the literature but the term ELL is used in this article.
2. ESL or English as a second language programs are also referred to as English to speakers of other languages (ESOL) programs.
3. See Lopez (in press) for additional details.
4. It was beyond the scope of this manuscript to address issues relevant to culturally sensitive classroom management strategies. Readers interested in obtaining additional information about culturally sensitive classroom management strategies should refer to Zirpoli (2005, Chapter 14).

REFERENCES

Baca, L. M., & Cervantes, H. T. (Eds.). (2004). *The bilingual special education interface* (4th ed.). Upper Saddle River, NJ: Pearson/Merrill Prentice Hall.
Baker, S. K., & Good, R. (1995). Curriculum-based measurement of English reading with bilingual Hispanic students: A validation study with second-grade students. *School Psychology Review, 24*, 561-578.

Borden, J. F. (1998). The pitfalls and possibilities for organizing quality ESL programs. *Middle School Journal, 29*(3), 25-33.

Brophy, J., & Good, T. L. (1986). Teacher behavior and student achievement. In M. Witrock (Ed.), *The third handbook of research on teaching* (pp. 328-375). New York: Macmillan.

Brown, D., Pryzwansky, W. B., & Shulte, A. C. (2001). *Psychological consultation: Introduction to theory and practice* (5th ed.). Boston: Allyn & Bacon.

Chamot, A. U. (1998). Effective instruction for high school for English language learners. In R. M. Gersten & R. T. Jimenez (1998). *Promoting learning for culturally and linguistically diverse students: Classroom applications from contemporary research* (pp. 187-209). Belmont, CA: Wadsworth Publishing Company.

Collier, V. P. (1992). A synthesis of studies examining long-term language minority student data on academic achievement. *Bilingual Research Journal, 16,* 187-212.

Cummins, J. (1984). *Bilingualism and special education: Issues in assessment and pedagogy.* San Diego: College-Hill.

Cummins, J., & Swain, M. (1986). *Bilingualism in education: Aspects of theory, research and practice.* London: Longman.

Denton, C. A., Anthony, J. L., Parker, R., & Hasbrouck, J. (2004). Effects of two tutoring programs on the English reading development of Spanish-English bilingual students. *The Elementary School Journal, 104,* 289-305.

de Valenzuela, J. S. & Niccolai, S. (2004). Language development in culturally and linguistically diverse students with special needs. In L. M. Baca & H. T. Cervantes (Eds.) *The bilingual special education interface* (4th ed.; pp. 124-161). Upper Saddle River, NJ: Pearson/Merrill Prentice Hall.

Echevarria, J., & Short, D. J. (2004). Using multiple perspectives in observations of diverse classrooms: The Sheltered Instruction Observation Protocol. In H. C. Waxman, R. G. Tharp, & R. Soleste Hilberg (Eds.), *Observational research in U.S. classrooms: New approaches for understanding cultural and linguistic diversity* (pp. 21-47). Cambridge: Cambridge University Press.

Ellis, R. (1994). *The study of second-language acquisition.* Oxford: Oxford University Press.

Gersten, R. M., & Baker, S. (2000). The professional knowledge base on instructional practices that support cognitive growth for English-language learners. In R. Gersten, E. P. Schiller, & S. Vaughn (Eds.), *Contemporary special education research: Synthesis of the knowledge base on critical instructional issues* (pp. 31-79). Mahwah, NJ: Erlbaum.

Gersten, R. M., & Jimenez, R. T. (1998). *Promoting learning for culturally and linguistically diverse students: Classroom applications from contemporary research.* Belmont, CA: Wadsworth Publishing Company

Gersten, R. M., Marks, S. U., Keating, S., & Baker, S. (1998) Recent research on effective instructional practices in content area ESOL. In R. M. Gersten & R. T. Jimenez (Eds.), *Promoting learning for culturally and linguistically diverse student* (pp. 57-72). New York: Wadsworth Publishing.

Goldstein, B. S. C., & Harris, K. C. (2000). Consultant practices in two heterogeneous Latino schools. *School Psychology Review, 29,* 368-377.

Gottlieb, M., & Hamayan, E. (in press). Assessing oral and written language proficiency: A guide for psychologists and teachers. In G. Esquivel, E. C. Lopez, & S. Nahari (Eds.), *Handbook of multicultural school psychology: An interdisciplinary perspective*. Mahwah, NJ: Lawrence Earlbaum.

Gravois, T.A., & Rosenfield, S. (2006). Impact of instructional consultation teams on the disproportionate referral and placement of minority students in special education. *Remedial and Special Education, 27*, 42-52.

Gunn, B., Biglan, A., Smolkowski, K., & Ary, D. (2000). The efficacy of supplemental instruction in decoding skills for Hispanic and non-Hispanic students in early elementary school. *The Journal of Special Education, 34*, 90-103.

Gunn, B., Smolkowski, K., Biglan, A., & Black, C. (2002). Supplemental instruction in decoding skills for Hispanic and non-Hispanic students in early elementary school: A follow-up. *Journal of Special Education, 36*, 69-79.

Hylander, I. (2003). Toward a grounded theory of the conceptual change process in consultee-centered consultation. *Journal of Educational and Psychological Consultation, 14*, 263-280.

Illinois State Board of Education (1999). *The language proficiency handbook: A practitioner's guide to instructional assessment*. Springfield, IL: Author.

Ingraham, C. L. (2000). Consultation through a multicultural lens: Multicultural and cross-cultural consultation in schools. *School Psychology Review 29*, 320-343.

Krashen, S. D. (1982). *Principles and practice in second language acquisition*. New York: Pergamon.

Leafstedt, J. M., Richards, C. R., & Gerber, M. M. (2004). Effectiveness of explicit phonological-awareness instruction for at-risk English Learners. *Learning Disabilities Research & Practice, 19*, 252-261.

Lopez, E. C. (2006). English language learners. In G. Bear, K. Minke, & A. Thomas (Eds.), *Children's Needs III: Psychological perspectives* (pp. 647-659). Washington D.C.: National Association of School Psychologists.

Lopez, E. C., Liu, C., Popoutsakis, M., Rafferty, T., & Valero, C. (1998, March). *An examination of process and content variables in cross-cultural consultation: A case study*. Paper presented at the National Association of School Psychologists Conference. Orlando, FL.

Lopez, E. C., & Truesdell, L. A. (in press). Multicultural issues in instructional consultation for English language learning students. In G. Esquivel, E. C. Lopez, & S. Nahari (Eds.), *Handbook of multicultural school psychology: An interdisciplinary perspective*. Mahwah, NJ: Lawrence Earlbaum.

Martines, D., & Rodriguez-Srednicki (in press). Academic assessment of bilingual and English language learning students. In G. Esquivel, E. C. Lopez, & S. Nahari (Eds.), *Handbook of multicultural school psychology: An interdisciplinary perspective*. Mahwah, NJ: Lawrence Earlbaum.

McCloskey, D., & Athanasiou, M. S. (2000). Assessment and intervention practices with second language learners among school psychologists. *Psychology in the Schools, 37*, 209-225.

Meece, J. L., & Kurtz-Costes, B. (2001). Introduction: The schooling of ethnic minority children and youth [Special issue]. *Educational Psychologist, 36*(1), 1-7.

Meyers, B. (2002). The contract negotiation stage of a school-based, cross-cultural organizational consultation: A case study. *Journal of Educational and Psychological Consultation, 13*, 151-183.

National Center for Education Statistics (2005). *Public elementary, secondary students, staff, schools, and school districts: School year 2002-03.* Washington DC: Author.

National Center for Education Statistics (2002). *Schools and staffing survey, 1999-2000: Overview of the data for public, private, public charter, and Bureau of Indian Affairs elementary and secondary schools.* Washington DC: Author.

National Clearinghouse for English Language Acquisition and Language Instruction (2001). *Survey of the states' limited English proficient students and available educational programs and services, 1999-2001 Summary report.* Washington, DC: Author.

Ordoñez, C. L., Carlo, M. S., Snow, C. E., & McLaughlin, B. (2002). Depth and breadth of vocabulary in two languages: Which vocabulary skills transfer? *Journal of Educational Psychology, 94*, 719-728.

Ovando, C. J., Collier, V. P., & Combs, M. C. (2003). *Bilingual and ESL classrooms: Teaching in multicultural contexts* (3rd ed.). New York: McGraw Hill.

Rhodes, R. L., Ochoa, S. H., & Ortiz, S. O. (2005). *Assessing culturally and linguistically diverse students: A practical guide.* NY: The Guilford Press.

Rosenfield, S. A. (1987). *Instructional consultation.* Hillsdale, NJ: Erlbaum.

Silva, A. E. (2005). *English language learner special education referral and placement outcomes in Instructional Consultation Teams Schools.* Unpublished master's thesis, University of Maryland, College Park.

Silva, A. S., & Rosenfield, S. (2004, April). *Documenting English language learners' cases in instructional consultation teams' schools.* Poster presented at the National Association of School Psychologists conference, Dallas, TX.

Waxman, H. C., & Padron, Y. N. (2004). The uses of the Classroom Observation Schedule to improve classroom instruction. In H. C. Waxman, R. G. Tharp, & R. Soleste Hilberg (Eds.), *Observational research in U.S. classrooms: New approaches for understanding cultural and linguistic diversity* (pp. 72-96). Cambridge: Cambridge University Press.

Waxman, H. C., Tharp, R. G., & Soleste Hilberg, R. (Eds.). (2004). *Observational research in U.S. classrooms: New approaches for understanding cultural and linguistic diversity.* Cambridge: Cambridge University Press.

Woodcock, R. W., & Muñoz-Sandoval, F. A. (2005a). *Woodcock-Muñoz Language Survey Revised.* Riverside.

Woodcock, R. W., & Muñoz-Sandoval, F. A. (2005b). *Woodcock Language Proficiency Battery Revised.* Riverside.

Zehler, A. M., Fleischman, H. L., Hopstock, P. J., Stephenson, T. G., Pendzick, M. L., & Sapru, S. (2003). *Descriptive study of services to LEP students and LEP students with disabilities.* Volume I: Research report. Submited to the U. S. Department of Eduation, OELA. Arlingtong, VA: Development Associates.

Zirpoli, T. J. (2005). *Behavior management: Applications for teachers.* Upper Saddle River, NJ: Pearson.

doi:10.1300/J370v22n02_04

Home-School Partnerships
with Culturally Diverse Families:
Challenges and Solutions
for School Personnel

Ena Vazquez-Nuttall
Chieh Li
Jason P. Kaplan

Northeastern University

SUMMARY. Home-school partnership is one of the important contributors to every child's learning. The changing demographics of the United States present an urgent need for home-school partnership with culturally diverse families. Traditional family involvement practices are challenged when working with multicultural families. The authors propose an ecological model as a possible solution, with an illustrative case study with Hmong parents. Examples of parent involvement programs that apply some aspects of the ecological model with culturally diverse families are presented. Future directions and recommendations are discussed. doi:10.1300/J370v22n02_05 *[Article copies available for a fee from The Haworth Document Delivery Service: 1-800-HAWORTH. E-mail address: <docdelivery@haworthpress.com> Website: <http://www.HaworthPress.com> © 2006 by The Haworth Press, Inc. All rights reserved.]*

Address correspondence to: Ena Vazquez-Nuttall (E.Vazquez-Nuttall@neu.edu), Chieh Li (C.Li@.neu.edu), or Jason P. Kaplan (kaplan.j@neu.edu), Counseling and Applied Educational Psychology, 203 Lake Hall, Northeastern University, Boston, MA 02115.

[Haworth co-indexing entry note]: "Home-School Partnerships with Culturally Diverse Families: Challenges and Solutions for School Personnel." Vazquez-Nuttall, Ena, Chieh Li, and Jason P. Kaplan. Co-published simultaneously in *Journal of Applied School Psychology* (The Haworth Press, Inc.) Vol. 22, No. 2, 2006, pp. 81-102; and: *Multicultural Issues in School Psychology* (ed: Bonnie K. Nastasi) The Haworth Press, Inc., 2006, pp. 81-102. Single or multiple copies of this article are available for a fee from The Haworth Document Delivery Service [1-800-HAWORTH, 9:00 a.m. - 5:00 p.m. (EST). E-mail address: docdelivery@haworthpress.com].

KEYWORDS. School partnerships, family intervention, home school collaboration, culture, ethnicity

Home-school partnership can be defined as "establishing and maintaining productive, working relationships between families and schools to facilitate children's learning . . . and the knowledge that children's academic and social growth occurs across multiple settings" (Esler, Godber, & Christenson, 2002, p. 389). Home-school partnership takes into account the belief that, to maximize a student's learning, all areas in which children develop need to be addressed. Over the last decades, the U.S. government has instituted policies and initiatives aimed at increasing the partnership between home and school. Some of these include Title 1, Elementary and Secondary Education Act of 1965, as amended by Improving America's Schools Act of 1994; and Parent Participation, Goal 1 and 8 of the National Education Goals Panel of 1998.

This article addresses issues related to home-school partnership when working with a culturally diverse student population. The importance of home-school partnership to students' learning is discussed, with a primary focus on culturally diverse families. Relevant research is reviewed and an ecological model for working with a culturally diverse population is proposed. A case study with Hmong parents is used to illustrate how the ecological framework can be applied to individual cases. In addition, examples of intervention- and prevention-oriented parent involvement programs that apply some aspects of the ecological model with culturally diverse families are reviewed. Finally, future directions and recommendations are discussed. We begin with a working definition of home-school partnership.

SCHOOL-PARENT PARTNERSHIP RESEARCH

Years of research have shown that parent/family involvement contributes to better student outcomes related to learning and school success (Davies, 1991; Henderson & Berla, 1994). Parent/family involvement can be conceptualized into three categories: parent involvement at home, parent involvement at school, and parent involvement at home and school. Research points to all three categories as having positive impacts on student outcomes. Based on descriptive studies across student grade and income levels, Christenson and Sheridan (2001) identified four important family variables related to student performance: structure, support, expectations, and enriching environments (see Table 1). These indicators "represent the idea that families can and do play different roles in supporting their children's learning. School personnel increase the probability of family involvement when they value each role and help parents see the importance or benefit of different roles for their children" (Christenson & Sheridan, 2001, pp. 53-54).

Parent Involvement at Home

Support for parent participation at home was demonstrated by Finn (1998) who analyzed how specific parenting practices, such as organizing and monitoring time, assisting with homework, and talking about school issues, were linked to resilience of students despite challenges such as poverty, minority status, or native language. Callahan, Rademacher, and Hildreth (1998) found that children showed increased academic performance as a result of parents attending sessions on how to help their children with homework. Moreover, Cooper, Lindsay, and Nye (2000) found that the nature of involvement was an important aspect. Active teaching was found to be more appropriate with elementary school children, whereas reinforcing autonomy was more effective for older students learning time-management and study skills.

Parent Involvement at School

Also important to achieving positive student outcomes is parent participation either through volunteering or attending programs aimed at teaching parents how to help their children with academics. Many families are eager to obtain better information from schools and communities in order to be good partners in their children's education (Epstein, Croates, Salinas, Sanders, & Simon, 1997). At all grade levels, most students want their families to be more involved and more willing to take action in assisting communication between home and school (Epstein et al., 1997). Promising outcomes have been documented in both mathematics and literacy when children's parents/families are involved in the educational process (Faires, Nichols, & Rickelman, 2000; Galloway & Sheridan, 1994). Effective interventions range from teacher's notes to formal training on how parents can help and work effectively with their children at home.

The need for parent/family involvement is essential beyond primary school grades. Keith et al. (1998) found that continued involvement has positive effects on high school learning as measured by grades, high-

TABLE 1. Varied Indicators of Family Correlates of Student Performance

Correlate	Indicator
Structure	• Priority given to schoolwork, reading, and learning. • Consistent monitoring of how time is spent. • Authoritative parenting style. • Development of a reflective problem-solving style. • Availability of learning materials and a place for study. • Delay of immediate gratification to accomplish long-term goals. • Routine for completing home tasks. • Regular communication with school personnel. • Attendance at school functions. • Parental knowledge of child's current schoolwork strengths and weaknesses in learning.
Support	• Parental responsibility to assist children as learners. • Encouragement and discussion of leisure reading. • Modeling learning by reading and doing math. • Positive emotional interactions. • Responsiveness to child's developmental needs/skills. • Expression of affection.
Expectations	• Expectations for child's success. • Use of effort and ability attributions. • Interest in and establishment of standards for children's schoolwork.
Enriching Environment	• Frequent dialogue. • Informed conversations about everyday events. • Opportunities for good language habits. • Orienting children's attention to learning opportunities. • Reading with children. • Monitoring and joint analysis of television. • Enriching learning experiences.

Christenson and Sheridan (2001, p. 55); reproduced with permission.

lighting the need for school programs and family involvement at the secondary level. Such programs will likely need to include training on how parents can nurture the goals and expectations of their child and foster communication with schools regarding their child's future plans.

Cultural values and norms also must be taken into consideration. Researchers (Lopez, 2001) have found that the way in which Hispanic parents/families are involved in their children's education is different from those of other families. Thus, the cultural values of the families have to be respected and considered when implementing parent/family involvement practices.

URGENT NEED FOR HOME-SCHOOL PARTNERSHIPS WITH CULTURALLY DIVERSE FAMILIES

Cultural diversity is an important factor when considering the 2004 United States census projections that reflect the rapid demographic changes of our nation. According to the 2004 United States Census data, diverse groups will continue to increase proportionately with the greatest growth coming from Hispanic and Asian groups, and a decline in the percentage of people from mainstream European groups. The old notion of "white" majority is being replaced by one of multi-ethnic composition with no real "majority group." Based on these projections, practitioners are likely to encounter ethnic diversity no matter where they practice. Changing demographics require greater practitioner engagement in culturally competent practice, including collaboration with multicultural parents.

According to the U.S. Census Bureau (2004), significant discrepancies between racial and ethnic groups in academic achievement exist, with African Americans and Latinos scoring substantially lower on achievement tests. Some scholars (Jencks & Philips, 1998) have identified socioeconomic status as a significant contributor to such "gaps" in achievement. Others (Viadero, 2000) argue that poverty is not the only factor, and that teachers' expectations, quality of education, parenting, stereotyping, test bias, and academic coursework, among others, contribute to the gaps.

Challenges in Research

Currently, there is limited research to inform us whether practices that work for mainstream families also work for multicultural families. Many studies do not report the cultural background of their samples, instead describing the samples generically and thus not reporting the specific cultural make-up of the sample population. Researchers are facing several challenges: (a) Lack of culturally and psychometrically appropriate instruments to conduct research, (b) acculturation differences among immigrant children and families, and (c) variations in spoken language which create language barriers. Many children in this population do not speak English when they enter school, have not attended Head Start programs, or even participated in child-care. Their parents have different levels of education, socioeconomic status and English competency.

Challenges in Practice

Many traditional family involvement practices are considered ineffective with families from culturally diverse backgrounds (Esler et al., 2002; Ortiz & Flanagan, 2002). Several issues need to be considered when developing or selecting parental involvement programs for families from diverse backgrounds.

First, the ideal for parental involvement has traditionally been based on the model of upper-middle class, suburban community schooling with a family structure comprised of a two-parent, economically self-sufficient nuclear family, a working father and homemaker mother. This model is not appropriate for all families today, especially for minorities (de Carvalho, 2001; Finders & Lewis, 1994). For instance, middle class-based programs, with accompanying assumptions of cultural deficit for those not meeting the standard, do not provide Latino and other immigrant families with the tools needed to help their children and empower themselves (Daniel-White, 2002).

Second, culturally diverse parents are given information of varying quality regarding how to help their children attain their educational aspirations (Casas, Furlong, & de Esparza, 2003). Third, parents often do not know what roles they should play in the home-school partnership. This may be due to their lack of knowledge about the U.S. educational system and the cultural and educational expectations of teachers. For instance, immigrants are overwhelmingly supportive of education as a springboard for future success (Lopez & Sanchez, 2,000). However, the length of time the family has been in the United States as well as their level of acculturation can affect parental involvement. In many cases, the child may be the language and cultural translator for the family and parents (Bemak & Chung, 2003), although such practice can produce conflicts and is not recommended.

Fourth, the concept and form of family varies from one culture to another. Members from the extended family in many cultures, for example, Chinese and Vietnamese (Lee & Manning, 2001; Nguyen, 2002), Native American (Hildebrand, Phenice, Gray, & Hines, 1996) and Puerto Rican (D'Andrade, 1995), often participate actively in child rearing. Also, extended family, relatives, older children, and friends often provide emotional and economic support for children in African American families that are headed by single parents.

Fifth, there is no formula that works for all in any given racial/ethnic group, because within each group, there are many between-group (e.g., nationality, tribal, political) and within-group (e.g., gender, socio-economic, acculturation level) differences (Li, 1998; Liu & Li, 1998). Although the use of cultural knowledge to understand a particular group of people may be valid in general, not every single individual from even the most circumscribed culture will display any or all of the features commonly associated with it (Ortiz & Flanagan, 2002). Thus, any stereotyping could harm the parent-school relationship. Misunderstandings often occur when we fail to include the multiple dimensions of each individual's ecological context.

AN ECOLOGICAL APPROACH
TO HOME-SCHOOL PARTNERSHIPS
WITH CULTURALLY DIVERSE FAMILIES

As stated previously, the changing demographics in the United States require new approaches to involving families in schools in ways that make them feel welcome and ensure that they perceive the importance of supporting their children in learning and developing academic and social skills. This challenge to schools, professionals, and government officials can be better met when using ecological systems theory (Bronfenbrenner, 1986) to conceptualize and provide services. Christenson and Sheridan (2001) in *Schools and Families* explain that, as posited by Bronfenbrenner, an individual is an inseparable part of an interrelated system composed of a micro-system, mesosystem, exosystem, and macrosystem. We use an ecological model to explain parent-school partnerships, placing the family at the central part of the system (from school, community, etc.) and in relation to the whole system. Figure 1 presents an ecomap that represents the conceptualization deemed most appropriate when analyzing family-school partnership issues and solutions.

As Figure 1 illustrates, all levels of the ecological system are important for understanding and intervening in parent-school partnerships. However, the macrosystem is of major importance when dealing with culturally diverse families. As Bronfenbrenner (1992) stated, the macrosystem encompasses the concept of "cultural repertoire of belief systems" (p. 228). In the case of home-school partnerships, the macrosystem includes political and governmental systems and agendas, community-based cultural values and norms, societal and community needs and priorities, ethnicity, language of origin, beliefs and attitudes. The microsystem or family (as depicted in Figure 1) includes number of children, nuclear or extended family, education of the parents, religion, cultural background, and other variables. The exosystem includes school activities, organizations, and facilities; professional and advocacy organizations; university and private educational facilities; community health and welfare services, social and mental health agencies, and the religious community and neighbors. The mesosystem represents the relationships

FIGURE 1. Ecomap

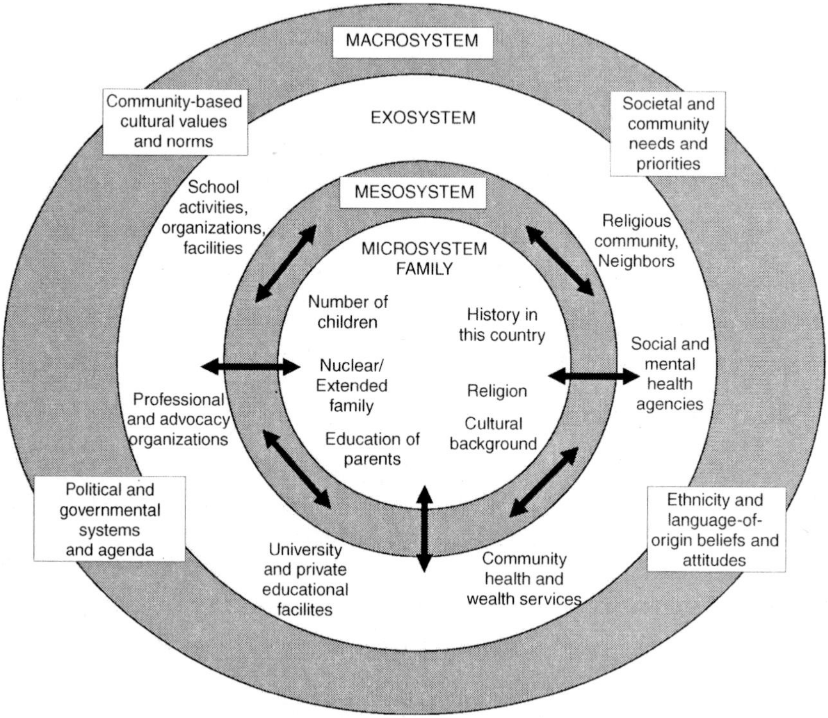

This ecomap was adapted with permission from Howard Knoff's (1986) adaptation of Bronfenbrenner's (1979) ecological model.

between the microsystem and exosystem, and their respective relationships with other components of the system.

"From an ecological perspective, home-school partnership needs to be viewed as within the entire community–its people and resources, its demographic across and between groups, its positive and negative interactions and the interdependencies among all these factors" (Raffaele & Knoff,1999, p. 452). Raffaele and Knoff (1999) emphasize that it is important for school personnel to be interested in the people and resources in their systems; to understand that there are four types of ecological interactions, positive, negative, neutral, and non-existent; and that these interactions are bi-directional. School personnel need to work on cultivating positive interactions. Raffaele and Knoff (1999) recommend a well-delineated strategic plan developed after analysis of the community's human, financial and political resources. The resulting procedural and managerial strategies can help prevent and solve the problems that impede successful home-school partnership.

Pianta and Walsh (1996) and Bronfenbrenner (1977) emphasize that children develop and learn in the context of the family and that shared meaning must be established over time between the child/family system and the school/schooling system. This statement is most relevant when one tries to understand research that reveals that some children fail in school because of the discontinuity between home and school (Pianta & Walsh, 1996). The following case study of family-school interactions involving Hmong parents illustrates how the ecological framework can be applied when home-school communication has broken down.

CASE STUDY: IMPLEMENTATION OF THE ECOLOGICAL APPROACH WITH A HMONG FAMILY

The following is an individual case study that applies the ecological and multicultural perspectives previously discussed. The case took place in an urban public school setting. The assistant principal, classroom teacher, and Hmong interpreter had been waiting over a half an hour for a conference with Kao's parents, recent immigrants from Southeast Asia. The assistant principal and the teacher became frustrated because the parents had already missed two conferences. The teacher was sure that the parents were informed about the conference as she had sent home a note in both English and Hmong. When the interpreter telephoned the home, she learned that the parents felt badly because they misread the time of the conference and rescheduled the meeting.

At the next scheduled meeting, the assistant principal and the classroom teacher greeted Kao's mother and father warmly and offered to shake hands with them. However, Kao's mother seemed reluctant to shake hands with the assistant principal while Kao's father seemed hesitant to shake hands with the teacher. Both of them avoided direct eye contact with the school personnel. During the conference, the assistant principal and classroom teacher did most of the talking. The parents just sat there listening to the interpreter. Their answers to questions were very limited, leaving the assistant principal and the classroom teacher wondering why the parents responded to them in this way.

Individual Case Analysis from an Ecological Perspective

From an ecological perspective, various levels of the eco-system in this case need to be considered, including cultural, linguistic, historical, individual style, and socioeconomic factors. At the macrosystem level, the recent immigrant Hmong parents should be seen in the socio-cultural context of their transition from an oral, agricultural society, to a post-industrial society with very different languages and customs. Based on their country of origin's history, they have been traumatized by wars, spent time in refugee camps, and been caught in the middle of severe cultural conflicts. Being in a new country, they have had to cope with many losses, including that of their homeland, family members, relatives, lifestyle and skills of which they were proud, and social status. They also moved from a relationship-oriented, collectivistic, agricultural society to an individualistic society which the Hmong parents know little about. These mismatches often create problems in a multicultural and multilingual urban school setting (exosystem). School psychologists are frequently asked to help figure out mesosystem problems such as the following: (a) Why some communication with parents and students do not work, for example, why parents do not come to a conference after the teacher has sent three invitation letters home; (b) why students or parents say "yes" to teachers but then do not follow through; and (c) how to solve these and many other problems.

In the case of the Hmong family, there seems to be a conflict of culturally influenced expectations and communication styles between school personnel and parents. The misunderstandings between teachers and parents also reflect typical communication problems caused by cultural and linguistic barriers. Kao's parents' limited answers to the teacher's and assistant principal's questions may result from multiple factors, for example, their cultural role expectations, their lack of knowledge of American schools, and language barriers. In this case, we do not know whether the interpreter even speaks their dialect. As the White Hmong and Blue Hmong can only understand half of each other's dialect, if the interpreter speaks a different dialect, then she can only translate half of the conversation. People from different cultures may use the simple word "Yes" differently based on linguistic differences (consistent with content vs. agreement with the speaker) and/or behavioral norm differences (trying to avoid arguing with authority).

Several other cultural and linguistic barriers are embedded in this case. For example, teachers expect parents to come to school activities or conferences and to help with homework. However, many Hmong parents do not read English or Hmong (they are from an oral culture), do not have formal schooling, and have difficulty finding babysitters. In addition, in mainstream American culture, teachers take shaking hands as a gesture of friendliness, but in the Hmong culture, women are not used to shaking hands with men. Making eye contact in mainstream American culture is expected in a conversation; in Hmong culture, making eye contact is not encouraged when communicating with an authority figure. In mainstream American culture, teachers expect parents to talk freely; in Hmong culture, teachers are seen as experts and authorities, and parents are expected to listen. All these cultural explanations may apply to the case of cross-cultural communication with Kao's parents.

The acculturation factor in the microsystem also needs to be examined. Parents, such as Kao's, who are at a lower level of acculturation, may be more likely to communicate in their ethnic style than peers at a higher level of acculturation. Thus, school personnel need to reach out to Kao's parents in a Hmong way. Furthermore, when discussing Kao's school adjustment issues with the parents, we cannot neglect the effect of acculturative stress. During the process of acculturation from Hmong to mainstreamed American culture, the Hmong family structure is changed partially due to the different pace of acculturation among family members, including learning English as a second language. Children often acculturate faster than parents because their attendance at American schools provides them with more opportunities to speak English and learn about the American systems. As a result, children often have to act as interpreters and liaisons between parents and school or community. These role reversals make parents, especially the father, lose power and authority. Very often, parents do not know what is going on in school and they are manipulated by the child, leaving the parents feeling powerless. It is often difficult for fathers to cope with the reversed roles in the family as they come from a patriarchal society. The child also can feel torn and frustrated because he or she often has to shift back and forth between the two conflicting cultures of home and school, a process which involves adjusting to different values, lifestyles, expectations, and concepts of children's rights. Awareness of such culturally related adjustment issues is crucial for working effectively with Kao and her parents.

Interventions from an Ecological and Multicultural Perspective

To improve the home-school communication and interaction (i.e., to solve the problems in the mesosystem), the school started by building multicultural awareness and competencies among school personnel (to bring changes to the exosystem) through the following interventions:

1. Providing a culturally competent staff member to consult with the school administrators and teachers and to share an ecological view of the presenting problems.
2. Conducting in-service workshops to help administrators, teachers, and other staff increase their cultural competency in working with Hmong people, including cultural knowledge, awareness, and skills. Teachers are encouraged to reach Hmong parents and students in a Hmong way, for example, by asking a Hmong-speaking teaching assistant to telephone parents in addition to sending letters home.
3. Encouraging school staff to gather information on Hmong culture through research and contact with Hmong children, parents and teaching assistants.
4. Encouraging teachers, parents, and students to learn from each other, mutually respect and adapt to each other, and organize multicultural fairs, breakfasts, or gatherings on topics of interest to parents, such as parenting in different cultures, coping with acculturative stress, etc.
5. Providing English classes for parents and Hmong language classes for children and school personnel, to bridge the communication gap.
6. Including the history and culture of Hmong in the curriculum, and ethnic story telling and writing in bilingual classes, to bridge the cultural gap.
7. Offering workshops to empower parents to work effectively with American schools on topics such as how U. S. schools function; school structures, rules, and responsibilities; requirements for mandated reporting by school personnel of suspected child abuse; rights and responsibilities of students and parents; free services and resources. In addition, providing workshops and booklets on living in two cultures and cross-cultural parenting.
8. Providing psycho-educational courses for bilingual/bicultural children to address the issues they are facing; increase their self-awareness, acceptance and appreciation of the self and others as bilingual and bicultural individuals; and improve communication skills.

Lessons Learned

The case study and review of literature indicate that, to strengthen home-school partnership, school personnel need to first understand children and their parents in their ecological system and then make school a welcoming environment (Hurley, 1999). School personnel also need to work at establishing continuities between home and school. Such continuities can be built through inviting parents to school, visiting families in their homes and neighborhoods, finding common values and interests that underpin mainstream and diverse cultures, and using them to bring home and school together. The next section presents examples of parent involvement programs that apply some aspects of the ecological model with culturally diverse families.

PARENT INVOLVEMENT PROGRAMS

In this section we describe several well-known parent involvement programs that are available for implementation in communities and schools. When investigating policies, practice and research in parent involvement programs, the National Council of Jewish Women (1996) highlighted four important considerations for program selection. First, few parent involvement programs for parents of children older than elementary school-age exist. Second, few parent involvement programs have been rigorously evaluated. Third, most parent involvement programs aim to change parents' behavior. Fourth, parent involvement programs for training teachers or changing the way that schools and parents interact are limited. Programs typically require parents to conform to school practices rather than training educators to accommodate to the cultures of the families or to incorporate the views of the parents. Considering these critical factors, the following parent involvement programs were chosen because they focused on parents and reflected the principles of the ecological model to a certain extent. Some of the programs concentrate on specific ethnic/racial groups, are available in different languages, and have been evaluated. Brief descriptions and evaluations are presented here. More detailed information can be obtained from the program developers (see contact information in Appendix A). Practitioners also are encouraged to conduct their own evaluation when using the programs in their respective sites.

School Development Program (SDP), one of the most well-known and widely used programs, was created by James Comer in the late

1960s in the New Haven, Connecticut, Public Schools. This program focuses on changing school ecology through three elements: (a) school governance system which includes parents, teachers, administrators, professional support staff, and nonprofessional support staff; (b) mental health team addressing the whole child (i.e., developmental and behavioral needs); and (c) parent program in which parents participate in social and academic activities at a comfortable level. Using an ecological model, the program's success is dependent upon the support of all individuals within the system and an understanding of parents' needs and views of education, and includes various definitions of parent involvement. The SDP has a substantial history of evaluation and research, both by its own staff and by outside evaluators. Comer Schools have been assessed on a variety of factors at different levels, including school climate, level of program implementation, and student self-concept, behavior, social competence and achievement. Studies of Comer Schools conducted by the SDP and by independent researchers have revealed significant effects on school climate indicated by improved relationships among the adults and students and better collaboration among staff (Comer, Haynes, Joyner, & Ben-Avie, 1996).

The Strengthening Multi-Ethnic Families and Communities program targets ethnic and culturally diverse parents of children ages 3 to 18. This program combines various proven prevention/intervention strategies that reduce violence against self, family and community. Program objectives include increasing parents' sense of competence and involvement in the community, and enhancing the child's self-esteem. The program includes five major components: cultural/spiritual values, rites of passage, positive discipline, enhancing relationships, family/community violence, and community involvement. Materials are available in English, Spanish, Vietnamese, and Korean, with a Russian translation in progress. Evaluation data from 22 parent groups ($n = 357$) show significant improvement in parents' sense of competence, family and parent-child interactions, and child competence. Data from over 1,000 parent pre-post questionnaires indicated an 83% overall program completion rate and 98% of participants recommending the program to others. Sixty-three percent of the program graduates reported increased community involvement, and 75% reported increased involvement in their child's school activities. Parents also reported significant improvement in their children's self-esteem and ethnic identification (Steele, Marigna, Tello, & Johnson, 2001).

In *Building Communities of Learners: A Collaboration among Teachers, Students, and Families,* McCaleb (1994) describes a program in which she applied the ecological approach to education and building partnership with parents. The program explores home-school cultural conflicts that young children experience through participatory research, in which teachers invite immigrant parents to the classroom for a dialogic process and co-authorship of family books. The process motivates both parents and children to play an active role in school. McCaleb (1994) evaluated the effectiveness of the programs through interviews with parents and qualitative analyses of parents' answers to a series of research questions. Parents' and children's responses were very positive. Raffaele and Knoff (1999) describe the benefits of the program, "In particular, McCaleb's program involves sensitivity to and respect for the cultural backgrounds of students and families, recognizes and values the important contributions parents have to make to the educational process, and engenders parental empowerment" (p. 461).

Massachusetts Parent Involvement Project (MassPIP), developed by the director Joel Nitzberg and his statewide staff, is a joint effort of the Massachusetts Department of Education, Museum of Science-Boston Institute for Teaching Science, Boston College, and Northeastern University. MassPIP's mission is to increase parent involvement in their children's mathematics, science, technology, and engineering (MST-E) education, with a particular emphasis on engaging and supporting parents whose children are underachieving in these areas, especially minority parents. As a result of the joint effort, 58 coalitions have been formed across Massachusetts. The strategic plan for these local coalitions included: (a) creating effective coalitions; (b) involving sufficient numbers of parents in coalitions; (c) developing parent leaders; (d) creating mobile activities to involve parents with their children in non-school settings; (e) providing information and extensions to activities used at home; and (f) evaluating and documenting the activities. Mass-PIP has been effective in getting parents involved in their child's education and in their child's school. However, it has been less effective in getting parents involved in curriculum policy in math and science, especially with parents of elementary school students. Although there was evidence across the state that some parents joined school councils and ran for school committees, there was limited evidence that parents were able to impact curricula changes and classroom instruction (Nuttal, Vazquez-Nuttal, & Landrum, 2001).

The Effective Black Parenting Program (EBPP) targets African-American parents of children ages 2 through 12 with the purpose of fostering family communication and combating juvenile delinquency, substance abuse, and other negative outcomes. This cognitive-behavioral program, specifically created for African-American parents, is taught by making references to African Proverbs which can be used for a variety of purposes. Some examples include, "He who learns, teaches" (Ethiopia) and "Talking with one another is loving one another" (Kenya). Using these expressions with the children enables the program's authors to recognize and honor the teaching strategies handed down from African ancestry. A 15-session program was field tested on two cohorts of inner-city African-American parents and their first and second grade children. Pre-post changes were compared in a quasi-experimental design with 109 treatment and 64 control families. Findings showed a significant decrease in parental rejection and an increase in both the quality of family relationships and child behavioral outcomes. A one-year follow-up indicated significant reduction in parental rejection, along with improvements in the quality of family relationships and child behaviors. There was evidence to suggest increases in social competencies in boys and parental mental health status, and decreases in delinquent behaviors among girls (Alvy, 1994). Over 2000 instructors have been trained and are using the program in schools, agencies, churches, mosques and Urban League affiliates.

Los Niños Bien Educados is designed to enable parents to assist their children with the challenges of growing up in the United States. Its aim is to help parents better manage their child's behavior and better relate to schools so that parents can take a more active role in their child's education. The program presents a wide range of basic child-rearing skills along with "*dichos*" or Latino proverbs used to make the learning compatible with Latino cultural traditions. For example, when discussing discipline, the program used the *dicho: A gran mal, remedio grande* (The greater the harm, the greater the remedy). Initial field testing for the program was completed in the 1980s with newly immigrated Latino families and was found to be very successful (Alvy, 1994). Since that time several other field tests have been conducted in various settings. Results from the Retrospective Assessment of Family Relationships Questionnaire showed that on average parents perceived their relationships with their children as much better following participation in the program; those who did not participate indicated that their parent-child relationships were the same or worse (Alvy, 1994). The program is currently used in several school districts and as part of dropout prevention projects.

In this section, we have briefly reviewed six parent involvement programs that are available for implementation in communities and schools. All of these programs apply some aspects of the ecological model with culturally diverse families. In conjunction with the case study, the programs bring the ecological framework to life. The next section addresses future directions.

FUTURE DIRECTIONS AND RECOMMENDATIONS

The changing demographics and review of research necessitate a reconsideration of approaches to parental involvement in education for culturally diverse populations. This section provides recommendations for future research, practice and policy.

Research

Based on review of more than 160 publications, Jordan, Orozco, and Averett (2001) identified four key issues for research and policy regarding family and community connections with schools: (a) clarifying concepts, (b) measuring outcomes, (c) advancing the research base, and (d) identifying critical areas of research. Jordan et al. call for increases in research-based knowledge as well as publishing and disseminating existing research evidence more widely.

A review of research on the effect of parent involvement in middle school student achievement revealed that effective programming required individualizing programs to meet the needs of the students, parents, and community (Brough & Irvin, 2001). Future work is needed to assist parents and families in learning how to create a home environment that fosters learning and how to provide support and encouragement for their child's success (National Council of Jewish Women, 1996). Furthermore, future work needs to take into consideration that parents may not know instinctively how to involve themselves in their children's education and may need to be taught how to create an environment that is encouraging and developmentally appropriate (Quigley, 2000).

Among the many questions that remain to be answered are the following: How should research studies be conducted with bilingual populations? Should study design for mainstreamed populations be replicated with diverse populations with translated or adapted instruments? Should studies focused on the children's culture be conducted with comparison samples from mainstreamed or other ethnic groups or only with their own group? Should new research designs be conceptualized?

Action

The authors agree with Raffaele and Knoff (1999) that to build a driving force for home-school partnerships at an organizational level, one should identify individuals and groups within the school system, home settings, and community who are currently facilitating successful home-school partnerships and could facilitate such activities in the future. Community businesses, social service agencies, after-school and childcare programs, religious institutions, government and civic agencies, and other grassroots organizations can nurture positive partnership between home and school. School systems should do an analysis of their schools, parents, and communities. If the school can identify cultural and linguistic differences, the school can then devise a plan to attract parents to school and to teach the children in more culturally appropriate ways.

Policy

The fast changing demographics of the 21st Century make the involvement of parents in education an imperative. National, state, and local governments need to formulate legislation requiring appropriate training and resources for family and school involvement. To establish true partnerships between parents and schools, the participatory model proposed by Nastasi et al. (1998) is worth considering. The model emphasizes a collaborative process in which partners work together to facilitate individual and cultural change. Partners should share information and decision-making. To remove logistical barriers to parent involvement, schools and local governments need to adjust current policies to make it possible for parents to meet with school personnel before or after school and to provide transportation and babysitting as needed. These factors need to be taken into consideration by educators and policy makers to help schools respond more effectively to the changing demographics of our nation.

CONCLUSION

Families of multicultural/bilingual backgrounds are increasing in number and are predicted to be 60% of the population by 2050, with no one single group representing a majority of the population (U.S. Bureau of the Census, 2004). It is imperative that school personnel at all levels, from pre-school through high school, learn how to inform diverse parents about American schools and how to help parents become involved in effective ways, thus providing children with learning opportunities both at home and in school. Teachers and supportive staff, including school psychologists, have to reach out to parents in their community and homes and welcome them in their schools. Effective parent involvement in schools is imperative if our nation wants to have well educated, productive, and effective citizens. The aforementioned ecological model appears to be a promising approach to home-school partnership with culturally diverse families.

ACKNOWLEDGMENT

The authors want to thank reviewers for their valuable critiques and Miss Florence Wong for her editorial assistance.

REFERENCES

Alvy, K.T. (1994). *Parent Training Today.* Studio City, CA: Center for the Improvement of Child Caring.

Bemak, F., & Chung, R.C.Y. (2003). Multicultural counseling with immigrant students in schools. In Pedersen, P.B., & Carey, J.C. (Eds.), *Multicultural counseling in schools: A practical handbook* (pp. 84-104). Boston: Pearson Education, Inc.

Bronfenbrenner, U. (1992). Ecological systems theory. In R. Vasta (Ed.), *Annals of child development: Six theories of child development: Revised formulations and current issues* (pp 187-249). London: Jessica Kingsley.

Bronfenbrenner, U. (1986). Ecology of the family as a context for human development. *Developmental Psychology, 22,* 723-742.

Bronfenbrenner, U. (1977). Toward an experimental ecology of human development. *American Psychologist, 32,* 513-531.

Brough, J. A., & Irvin, J. L. (2001). Parental involvement supports academic improvement among middle schoolers. *Middle School Journal, 32*(5), 56-61.

Callahan, K., Rademacher, J. A., & Hildreth, B. L. (1998). The effect of parent participation in strategies to improve the homework performance of students who are at risk. *Remedial and Special Education, 19*(3), 131-41.

Christenson, S.L., & Sheridan, S.M. (2001). *Schools and families: Creating essential connections for learning.* New York: The Guildford Press.

Comer, J.P., Haynes, N.M., Joyner,E.T., & Ben-Avie, M. (1996). *Rallying the whole village: The Comer process for reforming education.* New York: Teachers College Press.

Cooper, H. M., Lindsay, J. J., & Nye, B. (2000). Homework in the home: How student, family, and parenting-style differences relate to the homework process. *Contemporary Educational Psychology, 25*(4), 464-87.

D'Andrade, R. (1995). *The development of cognitive anthropology.* Cambridge, England: Cambridge University Press.

Daniel-White, K. (2002). Reassessing parent involvement: Involving language minority parents in school work at home. *Working Papers in Educational Linguistics, 18(1),* 29-49.

Davies, D. (1991). Schools reaching out: Family, school, and community partnerships for students success. *Phi Delta Kappan, 72,* 376-382.

de Carvalho, M.F.P. (2001). *Rethinking family-school relations: A critique of parental involvement in schooling.* Mahwah, NJ: Lawrence Erlbaum Associates, Publishers.

Desimone, L. M. (1999). Linking parent involvement with student achievement: Do race and income matter? *The Journal of Educational Research, 93(1),* 11-30.

Epstein, J. L., Croates, L., Salinas, K. C., Sanders. M. G., & Simon, B. S. (1997). *School, family, and community partnerships: Your handbook in action.* Thousand Oaks, CA: Corwin Press.

Esler, A.N., Godber, Y., & Christenson, S.L. (2002). Best practices in supporting home school collaborations. In A. Thomas & J. Grimes (Eds.), *Best Practices in School Psychology IV.* Washington, DC: National Association of School Psychology.

Faires, J., Nichols, W.D., & Rickelman, R.J. (2000). Effects of parental involvement in developing competent readers in first grade. *Reading Psychology, 21,* 195-215.

Finders, M., & Lewis, C. (1994). Why some parents don't come to school: Educating for diversity. *Educational Leadership, 51,* 50-55.

Finn, J. D. (1998). Parental engagement that makes a difference. *Educational Leadership, 55(8),* 20-24.

Galloway, J. & Sheridan, S.M. (1994). Implementing scientific practices through case studies; Example using home-school interventions and consultation. *Journal of School Psychology, 32* 385-413.

Henderson, A.T., & Berla, N. (Eds.). (1994). *A new generation of evidence: The family is critical to student achievement.* Washington, DC: National Committee for Citizens in Education.

Hildebrand, V., Phenice, L.A., Gray, M.M., & Hines, R.P. (1996). *Knowing and serving diverse families.* Englewood Cliffs, NJ: Prentice-Hall.

Hurley, C. (1999). *Welcome status and family school relationships: Perspectives of parents of ninth grade students with emotional or behavioral disorders.* Poster presentation at 1999 National Convention of School Psychologists, Las Vegas, NE, April 9.

Jencks, C. & Philips, M. (1998). *The Black White Test Score Gap.* Washington, DC: Brookings Institution Press.

Jordan, C., Orozco, E., & Averett, A. (2001). *Emerging issues in school, family, and community connections: Annual synthesis 2001.* Austin, TX: Southwest Educational Development Laboratory.

Keith, T. Z., Keith, P. B., Quirk, K. J., Sperduto, J., Santillo, S., & Killings, S. (1998). Longitudinal effects of parent involvement on high school grades: Similarities and differences across gender and ethnic groups. *Journal of School Psychology, 36(3),* 335-63.

Kessler-Sklar, S. L., & Baker, A. J. L. (2000). School district parent involvement policies and programs. *Elementary School Journal, 101(1),* 101-18.

Lee, G.L. & Manning, M.L. (2001). Treat Asian families right. *Education Digest, 67(4),* 39-45.

Li, C. (1998). Impact of acculturation on Chinese-Americans' life and its implications for helping professionals. *International Journal of Reality Therapy, 17*(2), 7-11.

Liu, T. & Li, C. (1998). Psychoeducational interventions with Southeast Asian students: An ecological approach. *Special Services in the Schools, 13*(1/2), 129-148.

Lopez, G. (2001). The value of hard work: Lessons on parent involvement from an (im)migrant household. *Harvard Educational Review, 71*(3), 416-35.

Lopez, L.C. & Sanchez, V.V. (2000). Immigrant and native-born Mexican-American parents' involvement in a public school: A preliminary study. *Psychological Reports, 86*(2), 521-525.

McCaleb, S.P. (1994). *Building a community of learners: A collaboration among teachers, students, families, and community.* Mahwah, NJ: Erlbaum.

Nastasi, B.K., Varjas, K., Sarkar, S., & Jayasena, A. (1998). Participatory model of mental health programming: Lessons learned from work in a developing country. *School Psychology Review, 27*(2) 260-276.

National Council of Jewish Women (1996). *Parents as school partners: Research report.* New York: Author.

Nguyen, T.H. (2002). Vietnam: Cultural background for ESL/EFL Teachers. *The Review of Vietnamese Studies, 2*(1). Retrieved October 5, 2005, from http://vstudies. learnabouthmong.org/onreslib1.html

Nuttall, R.L., Vazquez-Nuttall, E., & Landrum, V. (2001). *Final evaluation report: Massachusetts Parent Involvement Project (MassPIP)* Boston: Vazquez Nuttall Associates, Inc.

Ortiz, S. O., & Flanagan, D. P. (2002). Best practices in working with culturally diverse children and families. In Thomas, A. & Grimes, J. (Eds.), *Best practices in school psychology IV.* Bethesda, MD: National Association of School Psychology.

Pianta, R. & Walsh, D.B. (1996) *High risk-children in schools: Constructing sustaining relationships.* New York: Routledge.

Quigley, D. D. (2000, April). *Parents and teachers working together to support third grade achievement: Parents as learning partners.* Paper presented at the annual meeting of the American Educational Research Association, New Orleans, LA.

Raffaele, L.M., & Knoff, H.M. (1999). Improving home-school collaboration with disadvantaged families: Organizational principles, perspectives, and approaches. *School Psychology Review, 28* (3), 448-466.

Steele, M., Marigna, M., Tello, J., & Johnson, R. (2001). *Monograph: Parenting Styles and Program Impact Strengthening Multi-Ethic Families and Communities.* Los Angeles, CA: Consulting and Clinical Services.

U.S. Bureau of the Census (2004). *Projected population change in the United States, by race and Hispanic Origin: 2000-2050.* Washington, DC: U.S. Department of Commerce. Retrieved August 11, 2006, from http://www.census.gov/ipc/www/usinterimproj/

Viadero, D. (2000, March 22). Lags in minority achievement: Defy traditional explanations. *Education Week.* Retrieved August 28, 2002, from http://www.edweek. org/ew/ewstory.cfm?slug=28causes.h19.

doi:10.1300/J370v22n02_05

APPENDIX

Contact Information for Parent Involvement Programs

School Development Program (SDP), 55 College Street, New Haven, CT 06510, schooldevelopmentprogram@yale.edu

Strengthening Multi-Ethnic Families and Communities, Strengthening America's Families Project. University of Utah, Model Family Strengthening Program. Marilyn L. Steele, PhD, 1220 S. Sierra Bonita Avenue, Los Angeles, CA 90019

Building Communities of Learners: A Collaboration Among Teachers, Students, and Families. New College of California, 777 Valencia Street, San Francisco, CA 94110

Massachusetts Parent Involvement Project (MassPIP), Ena Vazquez-Nuttall, Ed.D., Northeastern University, 209 Lake Hall, 360 Huntington Avenue, Boston, MA 02115, and Joe Nitzberg, MEd, LCSW, Cambridge College, 1000 Massachusetts Avenue, Cambridge, MA 02144

Effective Black Parenting Program, Kerby T. Alvy, PhD, Center for the Improvement of Child Caring, 11331 Ventura Boulevard, Suite 103, Studio City, CA 91604, http://ciccparenting.org/

Los Niños Bien Educados, Kerby T. Alvy, PhD, Center for the Improvement of Child Caring, 11331 Ventura Boulevard, Suite 103, Studio City, CA 94604, http://ciccparenting.org/

Addressing Cultural Factors in Development of System Interventions

Chryse Hatzichristou
Aikaterini Lampropoulou
Konstantina Lykitsakou

University of Athens, Greece

SUMMARY. The purpose of this article is to address various issues concerning multicultural interventions at a system level. Diversity is presented through a different conceptual approach and specific implications for school psychological practice are addressed. In this theoretical context an alternative model of school psychological services that was developed in the Greek educational system is presented and a primary intervention program is described as a paradigm of multicultural system/community intervention. Finally, the components of a transnational approach to multicultural system/community interventions that provides the basic procedural guidelines to developing effective, culturally sensitive interventions in the school environment is proposed. doi:10.1300/J370v22n02_06 *[Article copies available for a fee from The Haworth Document Delivery Service: 1-800-HAWORTH. E-mail address: <docdelivery@haworthpress.com> Website: <http://www.HaworthPress.com> © 2006 by The Haworth Press, Inc. All rights reserved.]*

Address correspondence to: Chryse Hatzichristou, PhD, Department of Psychology, School of Philosophy, Panepistimiopolis, 15784 Ilissia, Athens, Greece (E-mail: hatzichr@psych.uoa.gr).

[Haworth co-indexing entry note]: "Addressing Cultural Factors in Development of System Interventions." Hatzichristou, Chryse, Aikaterini Lampropoulou, and Konstantina Lykitsakou. Co-published simultaneously in *Journal of Applied School Psychology* (The Haworth Press, Inc.) Vol. 22, No. 2, 2006, pp. 103-126; and: *Multicultural Issues in School Psychology* (ed: Bonnie K. Nastasi) The Haworth Press, Inc., 2006, pp. 103-126. Single or multiple copies of this article are available for a fee from The Haworth Document Delivery Service [1-800-HAWORTH, 9:00 a.m. - 5:00 p.m. (EST). E-mail address: docdelivery@haworthpress.com].

KEYWORDS. Service delivery systems, language development, school culture, psychology in schools

During the last decade, cultural issues in school psychological services delivery have constituted a subject of growing concern in the relevant literature. In the past, cultural factors have been examined mainly in relation to assessment and psychometric matters (Rogers, 2000), whereas little attention has been given to the impact of cultural diversity on the multiple aspects of school psychological practice. In addition, the current theoretical models and practices emphasize the need for a holistic approach to service provision in the school context that focuses on system interventions and enhances the collaboration among all members of the school community.

Experience and empirical data from planning and implementing such systemic interventions during the last years in Greece have evoked a number of issues concerning the applicability and effectiveness of models and approaches proposed and implemented in other countries and have urged us to consider the multiple dimensions of diversity apart from culture in order to develop interventions that respond to the needs of the specific system. Therefore, this paper addresses cultural factors from a systemic perspective and integrates elements from different theoretical models, methodological tools and paradigms into a unifying approach that could maximize the benefits of system-level interventions in different cultural settings.

In the following sections, an attempt is made to (a) develop a conceptual synthetic approach that addresses various issues concerning multicultural interventions at a system level from a number of different levels and perspectives; (b) discuss the impact of cultural factors on some of the roles of the school psychologist in providing various types of multicultural system interventions; (c) describe the development of an alternative model of school psychological services, providing an example of intervention in a specific cultural and educational setting, the Greek educational system; and (d) propose a transnational approach to effective, culturally-sensitive interventions in the school community, which attempts to synthesize different conceptual approaches and modes of implementation and to provide a set of guidelines for planning meaningful evidence-based interventions across different cultural and educational settings.

A CONCEPTUAL APPROACH
TO CULTURAL DIVERSITY IN THE SCHOOLS

Before attempting to approach the issue of cultural diversity it is necessary to differentiate among the terms in the relevant literature. There are many definitions of *culture* from different scientific perspectives. One of the most widely accepted definitions of *culture* is the one given by Triandis (1994) that refers to *culture* as a set of values, rules, ways of expression, religious beliefs and professional choices of a group of people that share a common environment and a common language. Culture is a global concept that refers to all human activity, whereas the term *ethnic* defines a group of people with a common heritage, language, religion, customs and values (Georgas, 2003). However, it is important to note that it is not just ethnicity, language and physical features but mainly the world views, experiences and perceptions that determine the existing cultural differences or similarities among people (Ingraham, 2000; Georgas, 2003).

In addition, it is important to differentiate among the terms *multicultural, cross-cultural* and *intercultural*. The term *multicultural* describes those environments within which culturally-related qualities are displayed. Many societies are characterized as multicultural because of the several cultural/ethnic groups that constitute them. However, it has been suggested that the specific term may not be as accurate as "polyethnic" or "plural" because members of nations interact, which leads to cultural diffusion (Georgas, 2003). In contrast to *multicultural* that describes diversity among cultural groups that co-exist within the same social context, the term *cross-cultural* refers to diversity across cultures in different countries or in the same context with minimum or no interaction (e.g., a student and his family who have just migrated from a foreign country). The term *intercultural* on the other hand implies interaction and has been used to define the approach and the procedure of intervention in multicultural contexts in order to enhance communication and promote interaction between culturally diverse groups. In this paper the term *multicultural* is used to describe the context of interventions (that is, the cultural diversity of the school community) in which intercultural actions and interventions are undertaken to promote cultural awareness and communication.

An *ecocultural* framework has been proposed by Berry (2001) in relation to cross-cultural psychology. According to this approach, human psychological diversity at an individual and group level is being studied in terms of two sources of influences, ecological/socio-political influences and a set of variables that links these influences to psychological characteristics. The Ecocultural Framework considers human diversity at all levels as a set of collective and individual adaptations to context (Georgas, 2003). According to Berry (2001) the specific framework "assumes a universalist theoretical framework in which basic psychological processes are taken to be species-wide features of human psychology, on which culture plays infinite variations during the course of development and daily activity" (p. 359). Therefore, culture should be perceived as just one of the determinants of behavior, adjustment and competence to be addressed within the general context of diversity when intervening in a multicultural setting.

Cultural Diversity and School Psychological Practice

The profession of school psychology is challenged to identify how and to what extent the basic domains of school psychological practice are adjusted in order to address cultural factors in the school community. Some important issues to consider when developing multicultural systemic interventions are briefly presented below. These include issues related to training and professional identity of school psychologists and the basic domains of school psychological practice, such as individual or group consultation and counseling, assessment and research, shaping educational and social policy, and program planning.

Consultation and counseling. Cultural awareness, understanding one's own and others' culture, is important in order to realize the way that cultural factors influence school psychological service delivery that could lead to increasing the efficiency of consultation/counseling and intervention practice. Cultural issues influence to a great extent the consultation process and it seems necessary to adjust the traditional process according to the needs and the cultural values of the consultant and/or the client that can be either an individual or a system. Values, beliefs, attitudes and even knowledge are largely defined by each one's cultural framework.

Cultural variables are important; and active inclusion and consideration of all participants' perspectives is needed in order to develop a theory for guiding cross-cultural consultation (Henning-Stout & Meyers, 2000). Tarver Behring and Ingraham (1998) have differentiated between *multicultural* and *cross-cultural* consultation. They define multicultural consultation as "a culturally sensitive, indirect service in which the consultant adjusts the consultation services to address the needs and cultural values of the consultee, the client, or both" (p. 58). On the other hand, *cross-cultural consultation* is a subset of multicultural consultation and it happens when consultation occurs across cultures.

As Ingraham (2000) points out, to date attention to cultural issues in school consultation is limited in the literature although the need for multi-cultural models and practices has been advocated within school psychology. She also proposes, as key aspects for the evolution of the relevant literature, empirical research and a comprehensive framework for the practice of multicultural school consultation that should (a) include a broad consideration of diversity; (b) attend to all parties in the consultation process; (c) consider the cultural context in which consultation occurs; (d) explore a range of issues related to consultation across and within cultures; and (e) identify competencies to develop and increase attention to areas in need of research.

Assessment and research methods. In the fields of assessment and research, cultural diversity has been considered as a substantial source of bias and error, inherent to the assessor/researcher and the assessment process/research methodology and tools. Culturally sensitive assessment should include (a) assessment of subjects' cultural orientation and identity (the extent to which the individuals or members of an ethnic group integrate or reject features of the dominant culture and/or of the culture of origin); (b) awareness of cultural bias in clinical diagnosis and assessment of personality and intelligence; and (c) emphasis on cultural validity in selection of instruments and interpretation of findings (Dana, 1993). Hambleton (2000) suggests four general domains that usually include threats to the psychometric qualities of tests that are being applied in different cultural contexts: (a) content, (b) test development and standardization, (c) administration, and (d) scoring and interpretation of the results.

Still, the issue of cultural competence of assessors, practitioners or researchers is a broader one. It is described as "the ability to provide services that are perceived by the clients as relevant to their problems and helpful for intervention outcomes. . . . It begins with acknowledgement and acceptance of cultural differences and it is based on experience and explicit training" (Dana, 1993, p. 220).

Shaping educational and social policy and program planning. School psychologists along with other professionals working in schools or for schools could provide empirically supported suggestions for appropriate policy adjustments, so that schools meet in the most efficient way the diverse needs of all students including those needs associated to cultural factors. Funding and incentives for in-service training for teachers and other school personnel are essential in order for them to gain professional development, cultural awareness and competence in dealing with diversity. Educational policy also should set as a priority curriculum adjustments that include positive examples against ethnic/racial stereotypes. It is suggested that any attempts for changes should start at an early stage, by enriching preschool and primary education curricula with appropriate goals, methods and material. Partnership between home, school and community is a significant factor that facilitates children's school adjustment and performance. Therefore, schools and community should make an effort to encourage parental involvement and also to facilitate families' access to community resources and supportive services according to their diverse needs (Christenson, 2004). Finally, state policy should include funding and other necessary means for planning, implementation and evaluation of intervention programs that address cultural diversity through a broader perspective having as a goal to promote children's mental health, positive school climate, involvement and collaboration of stakeholders from all ethnic and cultural groups of the community (Smith, Swindler Boutte, Zigler, & Finn-Stevenson, 2004).

Training and professional development of school psychologists. The development of professional competence is a multidimensional process, which requires extensive study and knowledge about multiculturalism and various cultural/ethnic groups combined with experiences in diverse settings (Barnett et al., 1995). The combination of knowledge mastery and practice is critical in providing opportunities for learning as well as self-reflection, development and change regarding personal attitudes, misconceptions, behaviors and professional skills. Hatzichristou (2002) has suggested common future perspectives and goals at a cross-national level associated with three interrelated domains: (a) collaboration of professional associations, (b) scientific foundation for practice, and (c) development of a multicultural professional identity. Training and continuing professional development have a decisive impact on the specialty definition, the roles of school psychologists, and the nature of school psychological services. Closer cooperation between national and international professional associations could promote specific action plans to develop: (a) opportunities for professional training (i.e., for school psychologists and teachers) and parent training programs; (b) guidelines for cross-cultural educational curricula that provide opportunities to share educational materials and include suggested readings, and to organize focused themes and training workshops, summer schools, etc.; and (c) multicultural professional training experiences (Hatzichristou & Lampropoulou, 2004). Cross-national collaboration that involves reciprocal knowledge sharing and personal reflection fosters our professional development and encourages a visionary and proactive approach for the evolution of school psychology worldwide (Ehrhardt-Padgett, Hatzichristou, Kitson & Meyers, 2004). The collaboration of university trainers, professionals, and students at national and cross-national levels is of critical importance in this effort as it provides new perspectives and offers opportunities to the field of school psychology to implement changes particularly in the context of community interventions.

Finally, another significant dimension of school psychological practice is *system-level intervention in the school community*. This is more thoroughly discussed in the following section in relation to cultural matters.

Multicultural Community Interventions

The term *community* refers to a network of relationships in which individuals with similar values and ideals are committed to shared objectives (Sergiovanni, 1994). The characteristics of the community are that its members care and support each other; they are strongly involved in its activities and decisions; they identify themselves with it; and they have a sense of belonging and share common norms, goals and values (Goodenow, 1993a, 1993b; McMillan & Chavis, 1986; Solomon, Watson, Battistisch, Schaps & Delucchi, 1992; Wehlage, Rutter, Smith, Lesko, & Fernandez, 1990). System-level intervention is defined as change efforts directed toward strengthening the feasibility, stability and/or functioning of an organization or system (Borgelt & Conoley, 1999).

In terms of multicultural community interventions, the development of cultural awareness and understanding that requires acknowledgement of similarities and differences between one's own culture and other cultures is an important prerequisite for effective system intervention within a multicultural context. Nastasi has proposed a Participatory Culture Specific Consultation model (PCSC) (Nastasi, Moore, & Varjas, 2004) that focuses upon identifying and addressing the culture-specific needs of individuals and systems. The key features of the PCSC are ethnographic research methods, action research process, participatory consultation process and cultural specificity. The model has been developed in nine phases, namely: Review of relevant existing theory, research, and practice; learning the culture; forming partnerships; problem and goal identification; data collection and problem-goal definition;

generation of culture-specific hypotheses; design and implementation of culture-specific interventions; evaluation of intervention and consultation; and institutionalization.

However, since a *system* is considered to be something more dynamic than the total of its components, it might be useful to adopt a *"metacultural perspective"* that considers multicultural systems as integrating the various elements of its consisting cultural groups into new dynamic outcomes. Research findings support this perspective since the majority of immigrant students have been found to follow integration as an acculturation process, which means that they preserve their identity of origin but at the same time they try to develop relationships with the members of the dominant culture (Giavrimis, Konstantinou, & Hatzichristou, 2003). However, the hosting culture is also submitted to change, and system resistance is initially to be expected. In order to restore the system's balance and functioning it is necessary for all groups to readjust their system of values, attitudes and beliefs. Therefore, the goal of systemic multicultural intervention on a primary prevention level is to facilitate this process, by helping all children surpass stereotypical perceptions and behavior, benefit from diversity and adopt a cross-cultural understanding and communication in the school environment. Thus, a culturally sensitive and not a culturally specific approach is essential in an effort to develop cultural awareness and understanding. Inevitably, an evidenced-based intervention that explores the needs of a specific system is the best way to ensure its validity and efficacy. This is also in accordance with the suggestions of most researchers and the current trends in school psychology worldwide that point out the need for empirically-based interventions along with the other services that school psychologists can offer (Kratochwill & Shernoff, 2004; Oakland, 2005).

Although culture is one of the most prominent dimensions of diversity identified in the school community that has attracted the interest of researchers and practitioners, it is not the only one that has critical implications for multicultural systemic interventions. The various levels of diversity have been presented in a synthetic approach by Hatzichristou, Lampropoulou, and Lykitsakou (2004). At the individual level, diversity is linked to the characteristics of the students (physical, cognitive, academic, personality, learning style, interests, etc.) and the teachers (personality, age, teaching experience, training, teaching style, etc). At the family level, differences are related to socioeconomic status (SES), structure and type, parenting styles, parental involvement, etc. Diversity regarding the school includes differences in school climate, communication, organizational-administrative and community parameters. Finally, in relation to service delivery, diversity refers to the implementation of different levels of prevention programs, universal or selective intervention, in-service training of school personnel, etc. Through this particular perspective, diversity is approached in a broader sense, including the various critical features that should be taken into account when developing interventions in the school environment.

Diversity as an Asset for Building Resilient Systems

One of the most current trends in the fields of research and social policy is the strengths-based approach that has emerged as opposed to the traditional deficits-based model. The latter focuses on difficulties, symptoms and problems of individuals, families or communities and seeks solutions by diagnosing, fixing, punishing or ignoring the ones affected. In contrast to this view, the strengths-based approach focuses on exploring and building on the positive potential of individuals or systems. For example, the deficits-based approach emphasizes tracking and remediation of less capable students; provides clinical treatment for children and adults with identified problems following expert- or government-defined prescriptions; focuses on negative emotions, cognitions, behaviors, traits and outcomes; tends to isolate, punish and pathologize families that are different; and views cultural differences as a problem for society. On the other hand, the strengths-based approach expects all children to succeed; capitalizes on child, teacher, and community strengths; emphasizes prevention of later development of problems by identifying and building on existing assets in individuals and communities; focuses on positive emotions, cognitions, behaviors, traits, and outcomes; supports all families and enhances family resilience; and values cultural differences and considers them as an asset to society (Maton, Dodgen, Leadbeater, Sandler, Schellenbach, & Solarz, 2004).

Building new strengths in individuals, families or in the community has been considered to have an important protective effect against adverse life contingencies (Masten & Coatsworth, 1998), and competence-based prevention programs have been found to prevent negative outcomes especially for high-risk children and youth (Durlak, 1997; Weissberg & Greenberg, 1998). Protective factors can be identified in various features of the individuals and their environment, and also are rooted in culture (e.g., traditions, beliefs, rituals and ceremonies, community support systems) (O'Dougherty Wright & Masten, 2005). However, the way in which these factors serve a preventive role is yet inadequately explored. It is hypothesized that even individual characteristics could be culturally influenced or interrelated. For example, cognitive, social or emotional skills could be associated with cultural demands and expectations according to the degree of cultural values and features such as individualism, collectivism, familism, world view, ethnic identity, and orientation (Gaines et al., 1997; Kim, Triandis, Kigitcibashi, Choi, & Yoon, 1994).

O'Dougherty Wright and Masten (2005) present a short list of resilience correlates with a protective function for children at various levels including community and culture. Community characteristics that foster children's resilience encompass high neighborhood quality (safe neighborhood, low level of violence, access to recreational centers, etc.), effective schools (well-trained and well-compensated teachers, after-school programs and school recreation resources), employment opportunities, good public health care, access to emergency services, and connections to caring adult mentors and pro-social peers. Similarly, cultural/societal correlates include protective child polices, values and resources directed at education, prevention of oppression or political violence, and low acceptance of physical violence. Longitudinal studies with high-risk children verify the protective function of supportive systems that counteract environmental threats (Coie et al., 1993; Doll & Lyon, 1998).

Classrooms can become resilient communities that provide support and guidance for all children. Based on findings of research on resilience, as well as educational and special education research, Doll, Zucker, and Brehm (2004) identified six characteristics of resilient classrooms: academic efficacy (students see themselves as competent and effective learners), academic self-determination (students set and work toward self-selected learning goals), behavioral self-control (students behave appropriately and adaptively with minimum adult supervision), caring and authentic teacher-student relationships, ongoing and rewarding relationships with classroom peers, and home-school relationships and collaboration (families know about and strengthen the learning that occurs in the classroom). Doll et al. (2004) also note that, according to systems theory, "neither the child nor the classroom can change without changing the other" and argue that "when the changes made by teachers, parents, and students complement and support each other, that change can persist and have an enduring impact on the routines and practices of the classroom" (p. 4). The following section describes an alternative model of school psychological services implemented in Greek schools that constitutes an effort to integrate the issues raised thus far as a means of developing effective community interventions.

ALTERNATIVE MODEL OF SCHOOL PSYCHOLOGICAL SERVICES

Considerable variability exists among countries regarding the role, function and training of school psychologists, the types of school psychological services offered, and the utilization of services (Oakland & Saigh, 1989). In Greece, the provision of school psychological services in mainstream public schools remains limited despite the progress that has been made in recent years. The lack of school psychological services in the Greek public schools constituted a unique challenge for the development of an alternative service delivery model in an effort to address the growing and unmet needs of different populations in the Greek educational system (Hatzichristou, 1998).

An integrative framework was proposed by Hatzichristou (1998) that synthesizes and expands the following conceptual domains: (a) the scientist-practitioner specialty in school psychology; (b) a systemic (i.e., social, cultural, ethnic, national, ecological) approach to assessment and intervention practices; (c) the evolving roles and functions of school psychologists in research, practice, and training; and (d) a systemic approach to professional development and identity of school psychologists. This integrative conceptual framework led to the development of a data-based model of alternative school psychological services linking theory, research and practice in the school environment aiming at the provision of alternative school psychological services including assessment, psychological consultation, prevention, intervention programs, crisis consultation, research, training, supervision, management and advocacy (Hatzichristou, 2004a).

The alternative school psychological services model was developed in four phases. The development and application of the model constitutes a dynamic process of adaptation, change, and evolution enriched by several new research domains and service components. A brief description of the four phases of the model is presented below.

Phase I: Profiles of "Average" Greek Students

The need to rely on an empirical data-base in order to develop effective intervention strategies is widely recognized. Therefore, a basic presupposition of the proposed model was the need for empirically-based interventions. The aims of the first phase of the model were to examine the following: (a) the profiles and normative patterns of competence across several domains of the "average" Greek students in childhood and adolescence according to the perceptions of teachers, peers and self; (b) prevalence and developmental trends of psychosocial and academic problems in the general school population; (c) the relationship between psychosocial problems and academic performance of Greek students; and (d) the effects of several independent variables (i.e., family status, city size) on children's functioning in schools.

Phase I was enriched by including new research domains with additional goals. The first research domain explored the perceptions and causal attributions regarding students' psychosocial adjustment and academic achievement using teacher, parent and student questionnaires. The other research domains included: (a) aspects of interpersonal relationships and communication between teachers and students; (b) classroom environment, school climate aspects, and support systems in the schools and family; and (c) school-family partnerships and collaboration (Hatzichristou & Hopf, 1991, 1992a, 1992c, 1996; Hopf & Hatzichristou, 1999).

Phase II: Profiles of At-Risk Students with Unmet Needs

Following the first phase, at-risk groups of students were identified using psychosocial, academic and socio-demographic criteria. The psychosocial and academic patterns of competencies were examined for the following groups of students: (a) peer sociometric status groups (i.e., popular, rejected, neglected, controversial); (b) students with learning difficulties; (c) migrant and remigrant students; and (d) children from single-parent families. The profiles of these groups of students with particular unmet needs were explored in comparison to all their classmates using teacher, peer and self-ratings.

The research domains were extended to include the following topics: (a) attitudes about divorce and perceptions of children's adjustment after parental separation according to students, teachers and parents; (b) school adjustment of migrant students; (c) children's rights; (d) health promotion in school; and (e) sex education programs

(Giavrimis, Konstantinou, & Hatzichristou, 2003; Hatzichristou, 1993; Hatzichristou, Gari, Mylonas, Georgouleas, Lykitsakou, Mpafiti, Vaitsi, & Bakopoulou, 2001; Hatzichristou & Hopf, 1992b, 1993; Hopf & Hatzichristou,1994).

Phase III: School- and Community-Based Needs Assessment

The third phase of the model included the exploration of the particular needs of specific school districts in a community where various intervention programs were being implemented. Community information was collected through multiple sources and using various techniques to identify specific characteristics and needs of the community (Hatzichristou, Karadimas et al., 2001). The multicomponent and multiperspective needs assessment procedures used in this phase were important in gathering information to determine the specific services that were most useful in this particular community and its schools, and in establishing the cooperation and involvement of members of a number of organizations (e.g., schools, children's institutions, community services) involved in the change process (Curtis & Metz, 1986).

A new research domain was included aiming at exploring teachers', students,' and parents' perceptions regarding the delivery of psychological services in different school settings and the roles of school psychologists (Hatzichristou, Dimitropoulou, Konstantinou, & Lampropoulou, 2002). This body of research revealed similarities with relevant research in other countries concerning the developmental profile and school adjustment and needs of students, but also particular findings for the students in the Greek educational system. These findings provided useful guidelines for the development of interventions in the Greek system, but also may have critical implications for the development of context-specific and evidence-based interventions and practice in other countries.

Phase IV: Service Delivery Model

The empirical data derived from the first three evolution phases of the model were integrated into a comprehensive prevention-consultation approach and included the eventual foundation of the Center for Research and Practice of School Psychology (CRPSP) in the Department of Psychology at the University of Athens (Phase IV). The goals of the Center are to (a) promote education, pre-service and in-service training for students, school psychologists, teachers and parents;

(b) foster University-schools-community services partnerships and collaboration; and (c) conduct scientific research and produce publications.

One of the main activities of the Center is the evidence-based development and implementation of primary and secondary prevention programs in the school community. The goal of these programs is to promote children's psychosocial adjustment and learning and to provide psychological support to students in schools and institutions as well as consultation to teachers and families. Examples of primary and secondary prevention programs are described in details in various publications (Hatzichristou, 2000; Hatzichristou, Gari, Mylonas, Georgouleas et al., 2001; Hatzichristou, Vaitsi, Dimitropoulou, & Falki, 1999, 2000).

Over the past years a primary prevention program entitled "Program for the promotion of mental health and learning: Social and emotional learning in schools" has been developed and implemented in many public mainstream schools in Greece and Cyprus aiming to promote children's mental health, cultivate their social and emotional skills, enhance children's self esteem, and create a positive climate in the school environment for all students (Hatzichristou, 2004b, 2004c, 2004d). The program integrates research findings along with recent theoretical approaches on counseling, consultation, multiple and emotional intelligence, and systems theory; implications of effective schools (Bickel, 1999) and resilience literature; and current trends that emphasize the importance of positive school climate defined by the type and quality of the relationships among the members of the school community. According to the latter perspective, schools are viewed as "caring communities" (Baker, Bridger, Terry & Winsor, 1997; Battistisch, Solomon, Watson & Schaps, 1997). The program's particular characteristics are the linking of current relevant theory and research with practice, adjustment to the needs of students in the Greek cultural and educational setting, emphasis on "normal" and not pathological behavior, and use of multidimensional and multi-method assessment (evidence-based intervention).

The program consists of ten thematic units that provide children with a variety of information and skills for building social end emotional competence, namely: (a) communication skills; (b) identification, expression, and management of emotions; (c) self-concept and self-esteem; (d) coping strategies; (e) conflict resolution; (f) diversity in culture; (g) diversity in individual, family and social characteristics; (h) learning/ study skills; (i) social skills; and (j) crisis management in the school environment. In this context, cultural diversity is viewed through a holistic approach as one of the levels of diversity, integrated in a broader program for the promotion of students' mental health. Thus, the focus was not simply to address cultural diversity but also to respond to the common needs and difficulties of all children by building various critical competencies such as communication, self-esteem, emotion management, and coping skills. This approach is supported by research findings that indicate that content-specific interventions (e.g., bullying, drug abuse, conflict resolution) are more effective when they are part of broader programs for the promotion of children's mental health (Coleman & Fisher-Yoshida, 2003).

Models of implementation and training. Throughout the years there have been different models of implementation of the program in an effort to correspond to the existing resources, the various needs of the target populations in the community, and the feedback from the evaluation process of previous phases of implementation. During the pilot phase the program was implemented by school psychologists, members of the scientific team of the *CRPSP,* whereas in the following years graduate students of school psychology and teachers undertook this task after a thorough specialized training and under the supervision of the Center's scientific team.

In its latest form of implementation in Greek elementary schools, the program was implemented by teachers and it was developed in an effort to promote children's mental health and to provide psychosocial support to students coming from different cultural contexts. The training and implementation process included the following phases: (a) selection of teachers (approximately 300 teachers, directors, and administrators were initially selected from schools with high percentage of migrant students); (b) general sensitization seminars on promotion of mental health and cross-cultural awareness and understanding (for all selected participants); (c) further specialized training for program implementation (approximately 80 of the teachers who attended the sensitization seminars were selected for the specialized training); and (d) implementation of the program in the schools and supervision.

The thematic unit *"Diversity in Culture"* was included in this particular program, placing special emphasis on addressing cultural factors that influence the psychosocial and academic adjustment of students in the Greek schools. The content and structure of the particular unit was based on foreign and Greek literature review, as well as research findings from the needs assessment phase that preceded the development of the program aimed at exploring Greek and foreign students', teachers' and parents' perceptions and needs in the Greek educational system.

An important part of program design and implementation is the evaluation of the program's validity and efficacy. The CRPSP has developed a multi-level assessment model including process and outcome evaluation, evaluation by teachers and students, pre-, post-, and during the program-assessment, and use of control group. Data were collected by different instruments and methods (questionnaires, diaries and logs, personal reports from teachers during the supervision process and activities and projects from training seminars and implementation of the program in the classrooms). Some indicative findings of this process were that the program was highly accepted by all participants (students and teachers). Moreover, a significant finding concerning the children was whereas all students rated the program very highly, students of different cultural groups referred to different kinds of benefits associated to their particular needs (Hatzichristou, 2004b). All these data constituted a valuable source of feedback for the improvement and adjustment of the program in future phases of implementation.

Indeed, an important characteristic of the alternative school psychological services model is its flexibility and the possibility it provides for integrating evaluation feedback from prior implementation phases as well as significant components of other models in order to develop a transnational approach to service delivery. This dimension is reflected in the effort that was undertaken by the scientific team of the CRPSP to link the alternative model with the problem-solving model implemented at the Invitational Conference on the Future of School Psychology and to adjust it to the needs of the Greek educational system. School psychology graduate students and teachers were trained to use the problem-solving model within the context of the alternative school psychological services model and the activities of the Center in order to develop action plans for meeting the needs of children, families and schools (Hatzichristou & Lampropoulou, 2004).

The whole effort provided a consultation framework for considering and understanding cultural and national issues regarding the provision of school psychological services. The cultural and national differences identified in all settings and professions should be taken into account because they have a deep impact on the consultation process and service delivery.

Linking the two different models that seem to have as common aims to promote school psychology and to maximize benefits for the school community has been an innovative and challenging effort that is still in progress. Future intentions of the CRPSP include further elaboration of this synthetic model with the integration of new conceptual and theoretical elements in order to maximize its validity and efficacy in multicultural systemic interventions that focus on the development of school and community networks and partnerships. School psychologists working in different countries can benefit from each other by sharing information about the effective and ineffective approaches to psychological services that they have used and by being aware of different paradigms, belief systems, and philosophies that operate in different cultural and educational settings (Hatzichristou & Lampropoulou, 2004).

A TRANSNATIONAL APPROACH
TO MULTICULTURAL SYSTEM INTERVENTION

Examining the described intervention approaches at a community level in various systems and cultures, similarities can be identified. These similarities could form the basis of a transnational model that provides the general guidelines for program development and planning and it is characterized by flexibility regarding the content and mode of implementation in specific cultural contexts. It is also characterized as multidimensional, evidence-based, multi-disciplinary, and system-oriented. The components of this model include (a) definition of conceptual framework, (b) model development, (c) program development and (d) program continuation and dissemination (Table 1).

The conceptual framework of this approach is based on consideration of the common and diverse needs of children and systems, and explores the various parameters of diversity at all levels including culture as one of these parameters. For example, in an intervention that aims to develop the social and communication skills of children it is important to identify not only the particular needs and characteristics of children of different cultural, societal groups, etc. (e.g., people from different cultural groups differ in the way they express their feelings, or in the amount of gestures or other non-verbal modes of communication, etc.), but also the similarities and common needs of all children regardless of other parameters (e.g., communication is a way of expressing feelings, ideas; people communicate verbally and non-verbally; etc.). In this context, model development includes review of existing literature (theories and research) and assessment of the characteristics and needs of the specific systems where the intervention is implemented. In the process of program development certain factors should be taken into account that determine the type and the extent of services provided, such as who conducts the intervention (community or state services, public or private in-

TABLE 1. Components of the Transnational Approach to Multicultural System/Community Interventions

---

Domains of Conceptual Framework

- Consideration of common and diverse needs of children and systems
    - Diversity in the school community [individual, family, school, community]
    - Cultural diversity and school psychological practice [consultation, assessment, intervention, professional development and identity]
- Integration of theories that are culturally appropriate, applicable and effective within a specific context and development of a synthetic conceptual framework

Domains of Model Development

- Literature review on interventions
- Baseline research/Creating a data-base/Needs assessment
    - Phase I: Psychosocial adjustment and developmental profile of average students
    - Phase II: Research on specific target groups (LD, migrant students, single-parent families)
    - Phase III: Needs assessment–"ethnography" of the system and the community

Domains of Program Development

- Intervener (university centers, community services, institutions, etc.)
- Forming partnerships–seeking available resources
- Selection of type and levels of intervention (selective, universal, primary, secondary)
- Program design (selection of target groups, goals and content of the program, methodology–problem-solving approach)
- Forming the intervention teams (school psychologists, graduate students, teachers)
- Training models (levels, structure, groups)
- Program implementation and supervision
- Program evaluation (pre-post assessment, integrity, outcome, process evaluation)

Program Continuation and Dissemination

- Creating school and community networks

---

stitutions, university center, etc.), what are the existing needs and limitations of service delivery in each country (available resources, level and type of school psychological services, policy, etc.), cultural and other demographic characteristics of the population, level of cultural awareness and openness to other ethnic groups, and the existing perceptions and attitudes toward psychological services delivery and forming partnerships with other community stakeholders. The next phase refers to program design, selection and training of the intervention teams, provision of supervision and program evaluation. Finally, creating school and community networks that function as supportive systems is proposed as a means of ensuring program sustainability and dissemination.

Some concrete strategies for applying the proposed approach are the following:

1. *Development of a synthetic conceptual framework.* Select theories and methods that are appropriate, applicable and effective for the system where the intervention is going to be implemented. Consider the common and the particular needs and characteristics of children from all cultural groups that exist in the specific system. Consider the impact of cultural factors on the various types of intervention that you plan to apply and make the necessary adjustments.

2. *Model development.* Review the relevant literature on system-level interventions. Develop a data-base or review the existing research data regarding the psychosocial adjustment of average students and of specific target at-risk groups (i.e., migrant students). Conduct an ethnography of the system (explore the needs and the characteristics of the specific school community).

3. *Program development.* Who conducts the intervention? University centers, community mental health services, school psychological services or institutions have different types of resources, modes of implementation and access to the school system and the community as well as different capacity to form partnerships with school community stakeholders. Select the type and level of intervention.

4. *Program design.* Use the problem-solving model to elaborate on certain critical issues of problem design such as selection of the target groups, the goals and the content of the program. Form the intervention teams and define their role in the program. Define the level and the structure of the training model of interveners. Implement the program providing supervision to the intervention teams. Design a valid evaluation process for assessing program outcomes.

5. *Program continuation and dissemination.* Create school and community networks that will commit to working on concrete future action plans regarding the continuation and dissemination of the program.

Such a model is above and beyond culture which is considered as just one of the many levels of diversity that should be taken into account when developing community interventions in multicultural contexts. This approach employs a "meta-cultural" perspective that disregards the "dominant culture" stance. Instead, it focuses on similarities of cultures and individuals (common needs and adversities) and builds on positive potential, competencies and strengths as a means of enhancing resiliency. Therefore, culture as well as all other levels of diversity is addressed not as a barrier, loss or problem but rather as an opportunity for development, gain and challenge. A choice is made in favor of the "normality of diversity" in contrast to the "diversity of normality." Thus, cultural factors should be addressed at all levels of school psychological practice in order to maximize its benefits for all students, their families and the community through a culturally-synthetic approach.

REFERENCES

Baker, J. A., Bridger, R., Terry, T., & Winsor, A. (1997). Schools as caring communities: A relational approach to school reform. *School Psychology Review, 26*(4), 586-602.

Barnett, D. W., Collins, R., Coulter, C., Curtis, M J., Ehrhardt, K., Glaser, A., Reyes, C., Stollar, S., & Winston, M. (1995). Ethnic validity and school psychology: Concepts and practices associated with cross-cultural professional competence. *Journal of School Psychology, 33*, 219-234.

Battistisch, V., Solomon, D., Watson, M., & Schaps, E. (1997). Caring school communities. *Educational Psychologist, 32*(3), 137-151.

Berry, J. W. (2001). Contextual studies of cognitive adaptation. In J. M. Collis & S. Messick (Eds.), *Intelligence and personality: Bridging the gap in theory and measurement* (pp. 319-333). Mahwah, NJ: Lawrence Erlbaum.

Bickel, W. E. (1999). The implications of the effective schools literature for school restructuring. In C. R.. Reynolds & T. B. Gutkin (Eds.), *Handbook of School Psychology* (3rd edition) (pp. 959-983). NY: Wiley.

Borgelt, C., & Conoley, J. C. (1999). Psychology in the schools: Systems intervention case examples. In C. R. Reynolds, & T. B. Gutkin (Eds.). *The handbook of school psychology* (3rd edition) (pp. 1056-1076). New York: John Wiley & Sons.

Christenson, S.L. (2004). The family-school partnership: An opportunity to promote the learning competence of all children. *School Psychology Review, 33*(1), 83-104.

Coie, J. D., Watt, N. F., West, S. G., Hawkins, J. D., Asarnow, J. R., Markman, H. J., Ramey, S. L., Shure, M. B., & Long, B. (1993). The science of prevention: A conceptual framework and some directions for a national research program. *American Psychologist, 48*, 1013-1022.

Coleman, P. T., & Fisher-Yoshida, B. (2003). *Conflict resolution at multiple levels across the life span: The work of the ICCCR.* www.tc.columbia.edu/ecccr/pcccrlifespan.pdf.

Curtis, M. J., & Metz, L. W. (1986). System level intervention in a school for handicapped children. *School Psychology Review, 15*, 510-518.

Dana, R. (1993). *Multicultural assessment perspectives for professional psychology.* Boston: Allyn and Bacon.

Doll, B., & Lyon, M. (1998). Risk and resilience: Implications for the practice of school psychology. *School Psychology Review, 27,* 348-363.

Doll, B., Zucker, S., & Brehm, K. (2004). *Resilient classrooms, creating healthy environments for learning.* London: The Guilford Press.

Durlak, J. A. (1997). *Successful prevention programs for children and adolescents.* NY: Plenum Press.

Ehrhardt-Padgett, G., Hatzichristou, C., Kitson, J., & Meyers, J. (2004). Awakening to a new dawn: Perspectives of the future of school psychology. *School Psychology Review, 33*(1), 105-114.

Gaines, S. O., Marelich, W. D., Bledsoe, K.L., Steers, W. N., Henderson, M. C., & Granrose, C. S. (1997). Links between race/ethnicity and cultural values as mediated by racial/ethnic identity and moderated by gender. *Journal of Personality and Social Psychology, 72,* 1460-1476.

Georgas, J. (2003). Cross-cultural psychology, intelligence, and cognitive processes. In J. Georgas, L. G. Weiss, F. J. R. van de Vijver, & D. H. Saklofske (Eds.), *Culture and children's intelligence: Cross-cultural analysis of the WISC-III* (pp. 23-37). San Diego, CA: Elsevier Sciences.

Giavrimis, P., Konstantinou, E., & Hatzichristou, C. (2003). Dimensions of immigrant students' adaptation in the Greek schools: Self-concept and coping strategies. *Intercultural Education, 14* (4), 423-434.

Goodenow, C. (1993a). Classroom belonging among early adolescent students: Relationships to motivation and achievement. *Journal of Early Adolescence, 13,* 21-43.

Goodenow, C. (1993b). The psychological sense of school membership among adolescents: Scale development and educational correlates. *Psychology in the Schools, 30,* 79-90.

Hambleton, R. K. (2000). Issues, designs, and technical guidelines for adapting tests in multiple languages and cultures. In Hambleton, R. K., Merenda, P., & Spielberger, C. (Eds.), *Adapting educational and psychological testing for cross-cultural assessment.* Hillsdale, NJ: Lawrence Erlbaum Publishers.

Hatzichristou, C. (1993). Children's adjustment after parental separation: Teacher, peer and self report in a Greek sample: A research note. *Journal of Child Psychology and Psychiatry, 34,* 1469-1478.

Hatzichristou, C. (1998). Alternative school psychological services: Development of a data-based model in the Greek schools. *School Psychology Review, 27* (2), 246-259.

Hatzichristou, C. (2000). Προγράμματα ψυχοκοινωνικής στήριξης μαθητών. Η ελληνική εμπειρία [Programs of psychosocial support of students. The Greek experience]. In A. Kalantzi & E. Bezevegis (Eds), *Θέματα Ψυχικής Υγείας Παιδιών και Εφήβων* (pp.35-56). Athens, Greece: Ελληνικά Γράμματα.

Hatzichristou, C. (2002). A conceptual framework of the evolution of school psychology. Transnational considerations of common phases and future perspectives. *School Psychology International, 23* (2), 1-17.

Hatzichristou, C. (2004a). Alternative school psychological services: Development of a model linking theory, research, and service delivery. In N. M. Lambert, I. Hylander and J. Sandoval (Eds), *Consultee-centered consultation: Improving the quality of professional services in schools and community organizations* (pp. 115-132). Mahwah, NJ: Lawrence Erlbaum.

Hatzichristou, C. (2004b). *Εισαγωγή στη σχολική ψυχολογία* [*Handbook of school psychology*]. Athens, Greece: Ελληνικά Γράμματα.

Hatzichristou, C. (Ed.). (2004c). *Πρόγραμμα προαγωγής της υψ χικής υγείας και της μάθησης: Κοινωνική και συναισθηματική αγωγή στο σχολείο* (εκπαιδευτικό υλικό για εκπαιδευτικούς και μαθητές πρωτοβάθμιας εκπαίδευσης) [*Program for the promotion of mental health and learning: Social and emotional learning in school* (educational material for teachers and students in primary education)]. Κέντρο Έρευνας και Εφραμογών Σχολικής Ψυχολογίας, University of Athens: ΤΥΠΩΘΗΤΩ.

Hatzichristou, C. (Ed.). (2004d). *Πρόγραμμα προαγωγής της ψυχικής υγείας και της μάθησης: Κοινωνική και συναισθηματική αγωγή στο σχολείο* (εκπαιδευτικό υλικό για εκπαιδευτικούς και μαθητές δευτεροβάθμιας εκπαίδευσης) [*Program for the promotion of mental health and learning: Social and emotional learning in school* (educational material for teachers and students in primary education)]. Κέντρο Έρευνας και Εφαρμογών Σχολικής Ψυχολογίας, University of Athens: ΤΥΠΩΘΗΤΩ.

Hatzichristou, C., & Hopf, D. (1991). Προβλήματα συμπεριφοράς και σχολικής επίδοσης μαθητών πρωτοβάθμιας και δευτεροβάθμιας εκπαίδευσης σύμφωνα με τις εκτιμήσεις των εκπαιδευτικών [Behavior problems and school performance of primary and secondary school students based on teachers' evaluation]. *Παιδαγωγική Επιθεώρηση, 14-15*, 107-143.

Hatzichristou, C., & Hopf, D. (1992a). Εκτίμηση της συμπεριφοράς μαθητών πρωτοβάθμιας και δευτεροβάθμιας εκπαίδευσης από τους συνομηλίκους τους [Behavior patterns of elementary and secondary school students based on peer evaluation]. *Παιδαγωγική Επιθεώρηση, 16*, 141-164.

Hatzichristou, C., & Hopf, D. (1992b). School performance and adjustment of the Greek remigrant students in the schools of their home country. *Applied Psycholinguistics, 13*, 279-294.

Hatzichristou, C., & Hopf, D. (1992c). Αυτοαντίληψη μαθητών πρωτοβάθμιας και δευτεροβάθμιας εκπαίδευσης [Dimensions of self-concept of primary and secondary school students]. *Παιδαγωγική Επιθεώρηση, 17*, 253-277.

Hatzichristou, C., & Hopf, D. (1993). Students with learning disabilities. Academic and psychosocial aspects of adaptation. *School Psychology International, 14* (1), 43-56

Hatzichristou, C., & Hopf, D. (1996). A multiperspective comparison of peer sociometric status groups in childhood and adolescence. *Child Development, 67*, 1085-1102.

Hatzichristou, C., Dimitropoulou, P., Konstantinou, E., & Lampropoulou, A. (2002). School psychological services in the Greek schools: Teachers', students' and parents' perceptions. *Symposium at the XXVth Annual International School Psychology Colloquium*, Nyborg-Denmark, July 24th-30th.

Hatzichristou, C., Gari, A., Mylonas, K., Georgouleas, G., Lykitsakou, K., Mpafiti, T., Vaitsi, A., & Bakopoulou, A. (2001). Προσαρμογή παλιννοστούντων και αλλοδαπών μαθητών: I. Σχεδιασμός και εφαρμογή ενός προγράμματος ψυχολογικής-συμβουλευτικής παρέμβασης. II. Αξιολόγηση του προγράμματος ψυχολογικής-συμβουλευτικής παρέμβασης [Immigrant and remigrant students adaptation: I. Application of an intervention program. II. Evaluation of the program]. *Νέα Παιδεία, 99*, 13-36.

Hatzichristou, C., Karadimas, E., Giavrimis, P., Dimitropoulou, P., & Vaitsi, A. (2001). Διασύνδεση αξιολόγησης και παρέμβασης σε επίπεδο συστήματος: Το παράδειγμα της συνεργασίας Πανεπιστημιακού Κέντρου Σχολικής Ψυχολογίας με Ίδρυμα της Χαρακμής [Linking assessment and intervention at a systemic level: The example of cooperation of the University Center of School Psychology with a children's Institution of Athens]. *Επθεώρηση Συμβουλευτικής και Προσανατολισμού. 58-59*, 193-212.

Hatzichristou, C., & Lampropoulou, A. (2004). The future of school psychology conference: A cross-national approach to service delivery. *Journal of Educational and Psychological Consultation*, 15(3&4), 313-333.

Hatzichristou, C., Lampropoulou, A., & Lykitsakou, K. (2004). Ένα διαφορετικό σχολείο Το: σχολείο ως κοινότητα που νοιάζεται και φροντίζει [A different school: School as a caring community]. *Ψυχολογία, 11*(1), 1-19.

Hatzichristou, C., Vaitsi, A., Dimitropoulou, P., & Falki, B. (1999). Παρεμβατικό πρόγραμμα πολυδιάστατης συμβουλευτικής υποστήριξης: Η εμπειρία του Κέντρου Σχολικής και Οικογενειακής Συμβουλευτικής και Έρευνας του Πανεπιστημίου Θεσσαλίς [An intervention program of multidimensional counseling support: The experience of the Center of School and Family Counseling and Research of the University of Thessaly]. *Επιστημονική Επετηρίδα «Αλέξανδρος Δελμύοζο'ς», Σχολή των Επιστημών του Ανθρώπου Πανεπιστημίου Θεσσαλίας* (pp. 45-64). Volos: University of Thessaly.

Hatzichristou, C., Vaitsi, A., Dimitropoulou, P., & Falki, B. (2000). Δυσκολίες μάθησης και προσαρμογής των παιδιών στο σχολείο: Οι αντιλήψεις των εκπαιδευτικών [Learning difficulties and adaptation problems of children in school: Teachers' perceptions]. *Παιδί και Έφηβος. Ψυχική Υγεία και Ψυχοπαθολογία, 2* (1), 32-47.

Henning-Stout, M., & Meyers, J. (2000). Consultation and human diversity: First things first. *School Psychology Review, 29*(3), 419-425.

Hopf, D. & Hatzichristou, C. (1994). Rückkehr in die Heimat. Zur schulischen und sozialpsychologischen Situation griechischer Schuller nach der Remigration. [The return home: The educational and socio-psychological situation of Greek pupils after remigration] *Zeitschrift für Pädagogik, 40*, (1), 147-170.

Hopf, D. & Hatzichristou, C. (1999). Teacher gender-related influences in Greek schools. *British Journal of Educational Psychology, 69*, 1-18.

Ingraham, C. (2000). Consultation through a multicultural lens: Multicultural and cross-cultural consultation in schools. *School Psychology Review, 29*(3), 320-343.

Kim, U., Triandis, H. C., Kigitcibashi, S., Choi, S., & Yoon, G. (Eds.). (1994). *Individualism and collectivism: Theory, method and applications*. Thousands Oaks, CA: Sage.

Kratochwill, T., & Shernoff, E. S. (2004). Evidence-based practice: Promoting evidence-based interventions in school psychology. *School Psychology Review, 33*, 34-48.

Masten, A. S., & Coatsworth, J. D. (1998). The development of competence in favorable and unfavorable environments: Lessons from research on successful children. *American Psychologist, 53*(2), 205-220.

Maton, K.I., Dodgen, D. W., Leadbeater, B. J., Sandler, I. N., Schellenbach, C. J., & Solarz, A. L. (2004). Strengths-based research and policy: An introduction. In K. I.

Maton, C. J. Schellenbach, B.J. Leadbeater, & A. L. Solarz (Eds.), *Investing in children, youth, families, and communities: Strengths-based research and policy* (pp. 3-11).Washington: American Psychological Association.

McMillan, D. W., & Chavis, D. M. (1986). Sense of community: A definition and theory. *Journal of Community Psychology, 14,* 6-23.

Nastasi, B., Moore, R. B., & Varjas, K. M. (2004). *School-based mental health services: Creating comprehensive and culturally specific programs.* Washington, DC: American Psychological Association.

Oakland, T. (2005). What is multicultural school psychology? In C. Frisby & C. Reynolds (Eds.). *Comprehensive handbook of multicultural school psychology* (pp. 3-13). New York: Wiley and Sons.

Oakland, T., & Saigh, P. A. (1989). Psychology in the schools: An introduction to international perspectives. In P. A. Saigh & T. Oakland (Eds.), *International perspectives on psychology in the schools* (pp. 1-22). Hillsdale, NJ, England, Lawrence Erlbaum Associates.

O'Dougherty Wright, M., & Masten, A. S. (2005). Resilience processes in development. In S. Goldstein & R. B. Brooks (Eds.), *Handbook of resilience in children* (pp. 17-37). NY: Kluwer Academic/Plenum Publishers.

Rogers, M. (2000). Examining the cultural context of consultation. *School Psychology Review, 29*(3), 414-418.

Sergiovanni, T. J. (1994). *Building community in schools.* San Francisco: Jossey-Bass.

Smith, E.P., Swindler Boutte, G., Zigler, E., & Finn-Stevenson, M. (2004). Opportunities for schools to promote resilience in children and youth. In K. I. Maton, C. J. Schellenbach, B.J. Leadbeater, & A. L. Solarz (Eds.), *Investing in children, youth, families, and communities: Strengths-based research and policy* (pp. 213-227). Washington: American Psychological Association.

Solomon, D., Watson, M., Battistisch, V., Schaps, E., & Delucchi, K. (1992). Creating a caring community: Educational practices that promote children's prosocial development. In F. K. Oser, A. Dick, & J. L. Patry (Eds.), *Effective and responsible teaching: The new synthesis* (pp. 383-390). San Francisco: Jossey-Bass.

Tarver Behring, S., & Ingraham, C. L. (1998). Culture as a central component to consultation: A call to the field. *Journal of Educational and Psychological Consultation, 9,* 57-72.

Triandis, H. C. (1994). *Culture and social behavior.* New York: McGraw-Hill.

Wehlage, G., Rutter, R., Smith, G., Lesko, N., & Fernandez, R. (1990). *Reducing the risk: Schools as communities of support.* Philadelphia: Falmer Press.

Weissberg, R. P., & Greenberg, M. T. (1998). School and community competence-enhancement and prevention programs. In W. Damon (Series Ed.), & I. E. Siegel & K. A. Renninger (Vol. Eds.), *Handbook of child psychology: Vol. 4. Child psychology in practice* (5th ed.) (pp. 877-954). New York: John Wiley & Sons.

doi:10.1300/J370v22n02_06

Multicultural Issues
in Evidence-Based Interventions

Colette L. Ingraham

San Diego State University

Evelyn R. Oka

Michigan State University

SUMMARY. School psychologists involved in the delivery of psychological and educational interventions face the challenge of identifying interventions that will work within their schools. The evidence-based intervention (EBI) approach has received attention as a promising way to identify effective interventions. The national Task Force on Evidence Based Interventions in School Psychology (sponsored by the American Psychological Association Division 16 and the Society for the Study of School Psychology, and endorsed by the National Association of School Psychologists) has developed coding criteria to review, evaluate, and identify efficacious interventions. This paper expands the work of the Multicultural and Diversity Committee of the EBI Task Force and offers direction for school psychologists in selecting and implementing interventions appropriate for their settings. We explore the meaning of EBIs in the context of a diverse world and discuss the cultural considerations that are

Address correspondence to: Colette L. Ingraham, Department of Counseling and School Psychology, College of Education, San Diego State University, MC 1179, 5500 Campanile Drive, San Diego, CA 92182-1179.

[Haworth co-indexing entry note]: "Multicultural Issues in Evidence-Based Interventions." Ingraham, Colette L., and Evelyn R. Oka. Co-published simultaneously in *Journal of Applied School Psychology* (The Haworth Press, Inc.) Vol. 22, No. 2, 2006, pp. 127-149; and: *Multicultural Issues in School Psychology* (ed: Bonnie K. Nastasi) The Haworth Press, Inc., 2006, pp. 127-149. Single or multiple copies of this article are available for a fee from The Haworth Document Delivery Service [1-800-HAWORTH, 9:00 a.m. - 5:00 p.m. (EST). E-mail address: docdelivery@haworthpress.com].

necessary to responsibly adopt an EBI perspective. The paper is organized into three sections where we (a) examine EBIs from a multicultural perspective, (b) describe recent advances in infusing a multicultural perspective into EBI work and the *Procedural and Coding Manual for Review of EBIs*, and (c) offer a set of guidelines for making decisions about implementing an EBI in a new setting. doi:10.1300/J370v22n02_07 *[Article copies available for a fee from The Haworth Document Delivery Service: 1-800-HAWORTH. E-mail address: <docdelivery@haworthpress.com> Website: <http://www.HaworthPress.com> © 2006 by The Haworth Press, Inc. All rights reserved.]*

KEYWORDS. Language development, school psychologists, evidence-based, school interventions, culture and ethnicity

Will this intervention work in *my* classroom? ~ I am willing to try *one* intervention, which would you recommend? ~ Everyone is using this new intervention in a neighboring school district and we'd like to use it too. What do you think?

Questions such as these confront school psychologists every day. Once assessments are completed, problems identified, and recommendations formulated, how are decisions made about how to intervene and which interventions to recommend? Working in settings with diminished resources, limited time, and pressure for greater accountability, how does one provide effective interventions to a variety of problems that span academic, social, emotional, and behavioral domains? Is an intervention that has been studied with a population in one part of the country appropriate to transport to a very different client population and setting? What issues should a practitioner consider when deciding if an intervention in the literature might be appropriate and effective in their own work setting? School psychologists need guidelines to assist them in (a) evaluating the usefulness of intervention research, and (b) making needed modifications to best address the unique cultural and contextual setting of their practice.

A national movement to determine the efficacy of treatments based on scientific evidence has moved beyond the medical and health care arenas and into psychological practice. Whether referred to as "evidenced-based interventions" (EBIs) or "empirically supported treatments" (ESTs), these approaches to evaluating and identifying effective interventions are increasingly being embraced by policymakers, researchers, practitioners, and the public concerned with educational and psychological issues (Kratochwill & Shernoff, 2003; Ollendick & King, 2004; Stoiber & Kratochwill, 2000). EBIs and ESTs have been heralded as promising ways to improve psychological and educational outcomes by identifying interventions that have clear and robust scientific evidence for their efficacy and effectiveness. The focus of this paper is to discuss cultural considerations that we believe are necessary to responsibly adopt an EBI perspective in diverse contexts. The term EBI, used in this paper, encompasses a broad continuum of interventions that includes prevention, early intervention, remedial interventions, and crisis intervention, and is the term adopted within school psychology (Kratochwill & Stoiber, 2002a).

The EBI movement comprises a variety of disciplines, professions, and organizations that have developed frameworks and criteria by which effective interventions may be identified. By defining what constitutes an EBI, standard criteria may be applied to determine whether the evidence supporting the efficacy of the intervention can be viewed as trustworthy. Proponents of the EBI approach view the identification of interventions with credible scientific evidence as essential for informing practice and improving outcomes. Examples of such projects include task forces established by the American Psychological Association (APA) Divisions 12 (Clinical Psychology) and 17 (Counseling Psychology), as well as the development of the U.S. Department of Education's What Works Clearinghouse (www.whatworks.ed.gov/) in 2002. The Task Force on Evidence Based Interventions in School Psychology was established in 1999 by APA Division 16 (School Psychology) and the Society for the Study of School Psychology (SSSP) and endorsed by the National Association of School Psychologists (NASP).

The EBI approach, however, also presents a variety of challenges (Christenson, Carlson, & Valdez, 2002; Gonzales, Ringelsen, & Chambers, 2002; Wampold, 2002). One critical question that looms over this work is *for whom* and *within what context* are these interventions effective? This question is vitally important and concerns how *transportable* and *generalizable* the studied intervention might be to other settings and contexts. To what extent can the intervention be transported beyond the specific population(s) or group(s) with whom it was found to be efficacious or effective? Careful examination of the EBI approach has raised additional questions that include: How do cultural factors affect the intervention's effectiveness when implemented in different settings and contexts? Is it possible for interventions to be universally effective, or are interventions effective with specific populations and within specific contexts?

Although there is a vast amount of intervention research, the process of reviewing, evaluating, and identifying interventions that meet the EBI criteria is still in the early stages. The result is that there are a limited number of interventions that have been identified as EBIs. Furthermore, there is more research on the *efficacy* (studied in highly controlled situations) of interventions than on their *effectiveness* (implemented in natural contexts). Practitioners can't wait until there is a substantial body of research with their intended populations and within their specific cultural context, yet our professional ethics advise that tools and interventions should be valid and reliable for the specific individuals with whom they are utilized (APA, 2003). What is available to guide psychologists in selecting interventions with a high probability of success when target populations, interventionists, and/or cultural contexts differ from those for whom data are available? What should practitioners consider when using research methods to evaluate the effectiveness of interventions in their own settings?

The purpose of this paper is to report on the latest work exploring multicultural issues in EBIs within school psychology and to offer direction for school psychologists in selecting, implementing, and evaluating interventions appropriate for their cultural settings. The paper is organized into three sections where we (a) examine EBIs from a multicultural perspective, (b) describe recent advances in infusing a multicultural perspective into EBI work, and (c) offer a set of guidelines for making decisions about implementing an EBI in a new setting.

EXAMINING EBIS FROM A MULTICULTURAL PERSPECTIVE

Practitioners know that the interventions they find in research articles and textbooks often need to be modified to be appropriate for different settings and populations. Discerning the transportability of EBIs requires that practitioners attend to both the shared and distinctive features of their own practice compared with the published EBI, and that they recognize which features matter. The cultures of the client, clinician, and society all affect the mental health and services available to individuals (APA, 2003; U.S. Department of Health and Human Services, 2001). Thus, it is vital to consider how the cultural characteristics of the context, clients, and practitioners may influence the transportability of interventions (APA, 2003).

How Do EBIs Fit with a Multicultural Perspective?

To evaluate the potential effectiveness of a published intervention, interventionists need to know with whom the intervention was used, who the interventionists were, and in what setting the intervention occurred. When an EBI is found effective with college psychology majors earning extra credit in an ethnically homogeneous university, can one predict that it would be equally effective with multi-ethnic, multi-lingual families in an urban school with a high percentage of recent immigrants from Africa, Southeast Asia, and Mexico? Clearly, a reader of research would need to know with whom and under what circumstances the study was conducted. An intervention documented as effective with one population may not be effective when the same intervention is used with a different client population or is delivered by an interventionist with a different level of cultural and clinical competence.

This raises several questions for the EBI movement, including what it means to be deemed "evidence-based" and what counts as evidence? Even when detailed manuals are available to guide intervention implementation, what is the accepted range of modifications that depart from the original manual? How much adaptation is too much? When does the intervention become *transformed*? When an intervention is transported to a new setting and transformed, is it still considered an EBI, based on the original empirical study?

The inclusion of a multicultural perspective in the EBI movement has been slowly evolving to address these questions. The medical origins of the EBI approach initially focused on obtaining empirical evidence through randomized clinical trials. This perspective, which focused on clinical settings and paid little attention to culture, has influenced much of the present EBI efforts. The focus of the EBI initiative has been on methodology and evaluating the adequacy of evidence that permits interventions to be used with confidence beyond the particular study. The value of this approach is that it affords a systematic evaluation of the technical merits of the research using a common metric. Such an approach, however, is by nature narrow in focus. It runs the risk of decontextualizing the research and stripping it of context that is essential in understanding its value, meaning, and validity. For example, one concern is how manualized interventions can incorporate the rich knowledge that interventionists have about the values, perspectives, and unique practices of culturally unique settings where a non-mainstream culture is prevalent, and highly diverse settings consisting of multiple cultures, worldviews, and frames of reference. Counseling psychologists have been at the forefront in addressing issues such as these (e.g., Quintana & Atkinson, 2002; Wampold, 2002). For example, Quintana, Troyano, and Taylor (2001) have proposed the concept of *cultural validity* to broaden the existing types of research validity. This concept, which is discussed more fully in later sections, is used to evaluate the appropriateness of the study's design, procedures, interpretation, and discussion for a particular culture. These efforts to examine the role of culture in intervention effectiveness exemplify the recommendations of Sue (1999), who has argued for a greater focus on issues of external validity and the need to carefully describe the research participants.

Some authors have suggested that EBIs are incompatible with a multicultural perspective because of EBI's primary emphasis on internal validity at the expense of external validity (Sue, 1999). Sue (1999) described external validity as the "extent to which one can generalize the results of the research to the populations and settings of interest" (p. 1072). Despite the fact that there is limited research with ethnic populations, the EBI approach is often used to yield conclusions about the universal utility of interventions. Sue cautioned that identifying treatments as efficacious on the basis of a narrow and limited segment of the population is problematic because it fails to attend to issues of external validity with regard to race, ethnicity, social class, and underrepresented groups. A number of researchers (Atkinson, Bui, & Mori, 2001; Hughes, 2000; Wampold, 2002) also have suggested that an incompatibility exists because of the focus on the intervention as the sole explanation for outcomes. Hughes (2000) observed that the EBI approach has focused on demonstrating the causal role of the intervention in bringing about change without sufficient theory to explain how and why the change occurred. Furthermore, Atkinson et al. (2001) and Wampold (2002) argued that the intervention is one of many factors that contributes to psychological well-being and that current approaches to EBIs fail, for example, to acknowledge the critical role that the healing context may play, particularly for ethnic clients. Shared characteristics between therapist and client (e.g., a common worldview and compatibility of beliefs about the causes of and solutions for psychological problems) are important in understanding whether and why treatments work. The primary emphasis on interventions in explaining outcomes, to the exclusion of other explanatory factors, can result in overestimating the importance of the treatment (Wampold, 2002). Wampold's research provides evidence that the client's experience of the intervention (i.e., the nature of the *healing context*), is a more powerful predictor of outcomes than the treatment per se (Wampold, 2001).

In school psychology, there is increasing recognition of the value of innovative research approaches to identify and develop evidence-based interventions. Kratochwill and Stoiber (2002a), co-chairs of the national Task Force on EBI in School Psychology in 2002, observed that, "A research perspective that examines the role of cultural diversity to EBIs will also likely require a rethinking of research design and interpretations" (p. 31). Recognizing these issues, the Task Force has been committed to finding ways to include a multicultural perspective in EBIs.

Cultural Specificity Hypothesis

Early efforts to address culture and EBI included the *cultural specificity hypothesis* (e.g., see Kratochwill & Stoiber, 2002a). This approach seeks to identify the effectiveness of a given intervention for use with individuals of a specific cultural background. Presumably, this would allow interventionists to know which interventions are effective for which cultural groups. Initially, the Task Force thought this might be a valuable way to attend to cultural differences in client populations (e.g., Kratochwill & Stoiber, 2002a). Current methods for doing this, and the assumptions underlying this approach, however, can be problematic. One approach is to calculate separate effect sizes for clients of a specific cultural background and to compare the effect sizes of different cultural groups. Computing different effect sizes may work statistically for group designs, but it may not be applicable for single subject and qualitative designs (Quintana et al., 2001). Furthermore, Wampold (2001) has cautioned that the cultural specificity hypothesis is fraught with both theoretical as well as methodological problems. The fundamental assumption of this hypothesis is that culture, as an independent variable, may interact with treatment. In other words, different treatments may be effective for different cultural groups. While it may seem logical to attribute this to the critical elements of the intervention, each intervention is *culturally embedded,* and it can be difficult to discern the critical factors responsible for the success (or failure) of an intervention.

A culture-specific hypothesis also begs the question of how culture is defined and operationalized. While a variety of definitions of culture exist, culture is essentially viewed as a "symbolic and behavioral inheritance" within a community of people (Shweder et al., 1998, p. 867).

Culture thus includes ways of thinking, ideas, beliefs, patterns of behavior, norms, and routines, and is transmitted over time, across generations. To capture such a complex construct by relying on demographic characteristics such as gender, race, ethnicity, economic status, geography and age, clearly oversimplifies people's cultural identities and ignores the variability within groups (Coleman & Wampold, 2003). A number of researchers (e.g., Quintana et al., 2001; Sue, 1999) have made a strong case for examining the deeper psychological and social variables rather than simply describing demographic variables. Reliance on proxy variables such as race and ethnicity, which do not express the variability in perspectives and experiences held by individuals of the same demographic description, increases the risk of drawing faulty conclusions. For example, when clients come with vastly different levels of acculturation, perceived power, and adherence to their traditional cultural or ethnic heritage, proxy variables mask the variability in the underlying psychological and socio-emotional influences on their approach, acceptability, adherence, and experiences with potential interventions. Additionally, attention to the *context in which interventions are applied* and the *mechanisms of change* may be more fruitful, especially when the intervention is unsuccessful.

Recognizing Cultural Influences in Intervention Research

Culture influences the entire research process (Ingraham, Oka, & Nastasi, 2004, 2005; Quintana et al., 2001). Culture forms the foundations from which we view the world, make sense of our experiences, and communicate with others. Because we are often immersed in our own cultural vantage points, it can be difficult to understand the profound ways in which culture and cognition are linked until we step out of our worldviews and explore the perspectives of those very different from ourselves. The preponderance of school psychology literature in the U.S. is grounded in experimental or quasi-experimental, scientist-practitioner, or problem-solving paradigms developed by people who are predominantly educated and acculturated in Western ways of defining knowledge and human behavior. Our culture and epistemological perspectives create a powerful context that shapes the questions we ask, the ways we seek to answer the questions, the methodologies we employ to pursue our inquiry, the tools we use to gather evidence, the rules that guide our collection and interpretation of data, and the ways in which we communicate our findings.

Practitioners and researchers all have an important role in recognizing the multitude of ways that culture is expressed throughout the research and intervention process. It is important that psychologists understand that there are both visible and invisible ways that culture affects all stages of research in published investigations, as well as in practitioners' ongoing evaluation of intervention effectiveness for their clients. Similar cultural considerations and methods of inquiry can guide researchers seeking to investigate EBIs and practitioners who are evaluating the outcomes of specific interventions within the context of their own client populations and settings. Within the EBI literature, Quintana et al. (2001) referred to *cultural validity* as the appropriateness of intervention research for given cultural groups. They described how cultural validity can be threatened or strengthened during the various stages of the research process. Ingraham, Oka, and Nastasi (2004, 2005) expanded Quintana et al.'s (2001) notion of cultural validity in their recommendations for attending to culture throughout the EBI research and intervention processes. To address culture in more meaningful ways, we propose beginning at a fundamental level by (a) attending to cultural issues throughout the research, review, and intervention process; and (b) making the cultural characteristics of the researchers, participants, and treatment providers more visible (i.e., giving greater attention to the cultural context and people involved with research rather than simply focusing on the treatment itself). These principles guided our recommendations to the EBI Task Force, as well as the guidelines proposed in this paper for practitioners in selecting and evaluating interventions.

Culture permeates the questions asked and the choices of inquiry. Who defines the problems to study and the problems for which interventions are created? Who has developed the theories that guide our understanding of the world, and what paradigms or worldviews undergird these theories? Making researchers' theoretical assumptions about the nature and treatment of mental health problems more explicit would be useful for readers in determining the extent of similarities or differences between the person who posed the questions and the participants. Careful and full descriptions (especially those that go beyond demographic characteristics) about the persons asking the questions, delivering the interventions, collecting the data, and interpreting the results need to be explicitly provided in reports of research. This may help to reduce inappropriate overgeneralization of the findings from one context to another. For example, when researchers investigate interventions that address externalizing behavior problems such as disruptive behaviors in school, for whom is this a problem? For whom is this an important and relevant question?

Methods and tools of inquiry are culture-bound. School psychologists are accustomed to critiquing and evaluating research methods for their technical adequacy, their reliability, trustworthiness, and accuracy. These methods, however, may have different meaning and practical effects with participants of differing cultural characteristics. For example, what is the evidence that surveys or coded observations are equally viable methods to use across people with different levels of acculturation, perceived competence, and worldviews? Are surveys that ask respondents to select a response from multiple options, or to rank order a group of preferences, events, or behaviors equally valid across the wide ranges of cultures and worldviews that are prevalent in U.S. school populations? Different belief systems, such as linear or dichotomous thinking, global or hierarchical thinking, and collectivist or individualistic orientations, can characterize different cultural groups and underlie their experience of mental health problems (e.g., Markus & Kitayama, 1991; Peng & Nisbett, 1999). People's understanding of what constitutes well-being or mental health problems, for example, varies among cultural groups (Thompson, Bazile, & Akbar, 2004). Attitudes about seeking help for mental health issues also vary among ethnic groups, including the importance of relying on family for mental health difficulties and degree of trust in the provider (Thompson et al., 2004). Thus, whether a client finds a treatment acceptable may have as much to do with their cultural conceptions of mental health as with the treatment.

Psychologists need to ensure that the methods they select are valid for the participants with whom they investigate and in the settings in which they will be used. It is important that researchers report enough information about the participants, the interventionists, the researchers, and the intervention setting so that readers can entertain hypotheses about the cultural validity of the research methods and tools used in a given study. Investigators need to achieve a balance between internal and external validity. Thus, researchers can describe the participants and the setting, including the location, prevalent belief systems, and key issues salient in the setting. When there are confounding variables that make interpretations about specific group characteristics imprecise, psychologists can and should articulate the factors that led to confounded results. Chambless and Williams (1995, as cited in Wampold, 2002) found that confounds, such as therapist/client ethnic matching, socioeconomic status (SES) of participants (and the ways race and SES often co-vary), severity of disorder, and location of treatment (e.g., home or clinic) made it difficult to interpret for whom the treatment was most effective and why. Sue (1999) proposed that researchers should think of ethnicity as a "distal and largely demographic concept," go beyond simple comparisons of different populations, and "explain what aspects of ethnicity are responsible for the differences" (p. 1076). For example, in a study of a parenting intervention with recent immigrants from Mexico, it would be helpful to know not only the race, ethnicity, language fluency, and acculturation status of the client and treatment provider, but also the degree of trust established with the client. The provision of more meaningful descriptive information is an important start to moving beyond demographic proxies for culture.

Rather than making assumptions about the universality of research methods and interventions, the assumption should be made that research and evaluation methods, data collection tools, and intervention effectiveness are *undetermined until shown to be valid or credible*. Sue (1999) stated that:

> Problems occur when the assumption of generality is made. Generality is a phenomenon that should be empirically tested. It is in the best interest of science, and it is certainly consistent with the tradition of scientific skepticism, to avoid drawing premature and untested assumptions. Moreover, when theories and models applied to different populations are examined, important ethnic and cultural differences are often found. (p. 1074)

Interpersonal and cross-cultural issues between participants, interventionists, and researchers can influence the results, and researchers should consider and report the characteristics of these groups. Wampold (2002) argued that both the provider and participants of the intervention, particularly for diverse populations, are critical to describe and report. For example, a study that involved 93% children of white European American college students conducted in a large Kansas university should report these descriptive features and describe who the other 7% of the participants were. Until shown otherwise, we must entertain the hypothesis that the children of white college students in Kansas might respond differently to an intervention than children of Spanish-speaking migrant workers in the south of Texas.

Culture influences how we make sense of results of investigations. The rules that guide the coding, organization, and interpretation of data are defined by what we know and how we know it. They guide our selection of the features of the study on which we focus and those we dismiss. Which data are analyzed and which are deleted or dismissed as random or meaningless? How do we know if some unique scores are just outliers or if they represent a minority perspective that we should explore further? When we obtain limited responses from an interviewee, is it because the question asked for information the interviewee viewed as private or because our questions reveal a belief system different from the interviewee's? Perhaps they couldn't conceptualize the issues in the format or style asked by the researchers. How do we know if the interpretations developed by the researchers match with the meaning intended by the respondents? A qualitative methods technique called *member checking* is specifically designed to address this volume. Member checking is a process for assuring that the research participants' views inform the interpretation of data. Researchers check with participants as hypotheses are developed and interpretations formed to see if the new understandings are consistent with the perspectives of participants. Member checking is rarely used within most group or single participant designs; thus it is unclear how these research designs regularly address the potential misinterpretation of responses.

Researchers can improve the availability of research that is useful to practitioners and policy-makers in several ways. First, researchers can accurately report how they treated the data, what decisions were made about whom, and what to include and exclude for analyses. Until this is done, it will be difficult for readers to entertain hypotheses of what might be missing or obscured in a given research report. Second, researchers should discuss if and how the results and interpretations of findings were shared with participants, carefully describing any attempts to involve participants in interpretive processes. This is critical when researchers hold different cultural perspectives than those they are studying. There are a variety of participatory methods for accomplishing this (e.g., Nastasi, Moore, & Varjas, 2004). Third, attention to issues of external validity is needed. Sue (1999) noted, "It is my belief that internal and external validity are not equal partners, and that if we have erred, it is in the direction of attention to internal rather than external validity in psychological science" (p. 1072). Future research needs to include equal attention to both internal and external validity in the design and reporting of findings. As a step in this direction, we recommended elevating the importance of and evaluating external validity criteria in the next revision of the school psychology EBI coding framework.

RECENT ADVANCES
IN INFUSING A MULTICULTURAL PERSPECTIVE
INTO EBI WORK

Practitioners will benefit from the contributions of three relatively recent ways that multicultural perspectives are being integrated with EBI work: a growing emphasis on exploring the *causal mechanisms* of interventions, focusing on the nature of the *therapeutic context* (such as the providers of interventions), and examining *cultural validity* to evaluate the appropriateness of interventions for diverse populations.

What Matters: Examining Why Interventions Work

A clear understanding of *why* the intervention worked is critical to the responsible and appropriate extension of interventions to new contexts and populations (Hughes, 2000). It is not sufficient to simply demonstrate that a treatment resulted in significant improvements in clients. It is critical for research to be clearly grounded in a theoretical framework that allows for the precise identification of the causal mechanism. This will be more useful in determining whether it might work with new populations. For example, knowing that the critical mechanism for reduction in the client's aggression was the shift in interpretation of hostility may help to determine whether this type of shift might be plausible for individuals with differing cultural backgrounds.

The Nature of the Therapeutic Context

Although much of the EST/EBI research focuses on the treatment itself, a growing body of research has indicated that much of the variability in outcome may be attributed to characteristics of the healing context such as the *provider of the intervention* rather than to the intervention itself (Serlin, Wampold, & Levin, 2003). Variability among providers is often ignored in research; Wampold (2002) noted that therapists' effects accounted for nine times more variance than treatment effects in the adult psychotherapy research. This finding has particular relevance for clients of color, for whom therapist-client relationships, rapport, and trust may be more in question. Quintana and Atkinson (2002) noted that research should shift to greater focus on relationship variables and "identifying the cultural variables that maximize client expectations for problem resolution, client-counselor working alliance, treatment effectiveness, and other factors common across all treatments" (p. 289).

Considering Cultural Validity

The term *cultural validity* is used to express the aspects of validity that make research appropriate for members of given cultures. Quintana et al. (2001) proposed that cultural validity be added to and considered along with the other kinds of research validity: internal, external, construct, hypotheses and statistical conclusions. According to Quintana et al. (2001), cultural validity is needed because the "five articulated research validities fail to address the appropriateness of the research with respect to the cultural nature of the investigation" (p. 616). They define cultural validity as:

> The authentic *representation* of the cultural nature of the research in terms of how constructs are operationalized, participants are recruited, hypotheses are formulated, study procedures are adapted, responses are analyzed, and results are interpreted for a particular cultural group as well as the *usefulness* of the research for its instructional utility in educating readers about the cultural group being investigated, its practical utility in yielding practice as well as theoretical implications about the cultural group, and its service utility in "giving back" to the community in important ways. (p. 617)

Quintana et al. (2001) offered many suggestions for increasing the cultural validity of research, starting with the study design, procedures, and continuing through the interpretation and discussion of results. They outlined a series of considerations during the planning phase of research, in the measurement instruments, participant recruitment, data analyses, and interpretation of results. For each phase of the research process, they list potential threats to cultural validity and corresponding ways to improve cultural validity. The conceptualization and operationalization of cultural validity has much to offer in research and reviewing of research in school psychology. The inclusion of cultural validity is an important way to address the effectiveness and relevance of EBIs for diverse populations and contexts of practice.

Integrating Cultural Diversity and Methodological Diversity into the EBI Movement

The Task Force in Evidence-Based Interventions in School Psychology has focused on developing conceptual definitions, criteria, and a comprehensive *Procedural and Coding Manual for Review of Evidence-Based Interventions* to evaluate and identify effective interventions across several domains of school psychology (Kratochwill & Stoiber, 2000, 2002a; Stoiber & Kratochwill, 2000). As part of this Task Force, Oka and Ingraham co-chaired a committee that was charged with providing guidance to the Task Force related to issues of cultural diversity. Ingraham, Oka, and Nastasi (2004, 2005) transformed Quintana et al.'s (2001) cultural validity dimensions into items that could be coded within each of the components of the research process, and we proposed revisions to the manual to bring external validity issues into greater prominence. For example, we developed new items to evaluate the thoroughness of descriptions of the interveners and researchers, expanded the evaluation of participant descriptions, focused on the representativeness of a participant sample compared with the larger population, and developed a new code to evaluate the transferability of an intervention. The proposal is now under consideration by the Task Force for inclusion in the next revision of the school psychology *Procedural and Coding Manual.*

GUIDELINES FOR MAKING DECISIONS ABOUT IMPLEMENTING AN EBI IN A NEW SETTING

Policy-makers and practitioners who are studying various EBIs for potential use within their own cultural and environmental context need to assess two central factors: (a) the quality of evidence available to support a given intervention; and perhaps even more importantly, (b) the generalizability and transferability of the given intervention to their intended setting and context. Once an intervention is selected for use in a new context, use of a scientist-practitioner approach can suggest appropriate ways to collect data, evaluate the efficacy of the intervention in the new context, and make modifications as needed.

Assessing the Quality of Evidence Available

The first step can be accomplished by considering research reviews that use the most recent version of the *Procedural and Coding Manual for Review of Evidence-Based Intervention.* This manual provides a comprehensive range of items for evaluating the scientific merits of a study using the criteria derived through several years of work by a national panel of experts (Kratochwill & Stoiber, 2002a, 2002b). Our proposed revision of the manual provides (a) greater articulation and inclusion of items for interventions relevant to culturally diverse settings, and (b) criteria for studies that use quantitative, qualitative, and mixed-methods designs. In addition, the manual can provide guidance to researchers and practitioners who want to use the best science to design, evaluate, and document evidence for school psychology interventions.

Studying the Generalizability and Transferability of an Intervention

Is the intervention culture-specific or universal? Can it be used with participants of different cultural backgrounds? Can the intervention be adopted in different settings and contexts? Sue (1998) noted that the ability to know when to generalize versus when to individualize is a critical component of cultural competence. Studying the transferability and generalizability of a given intervention is central to making decisions about if and how to replicate or adopt the intervention approach in a new setting. Transferability assessments are critical in the transportation of interventions across settings and participant populations.

For example, decision-makers reading research about a particular social skills intervention need to know if the study results show that it was designed for use with a specific cultural population, and to be delivered by interventionists with specified types of training and characteristics. They need to compare the characteristics of their own student population, interventionists, and setting, with those in the study. They also need to consider who will need training, what the process should be for training these interventionists, and with whom the intervention is likely to work and not work. Only then will they be able to decide, for example, if the district should invest in the intervention program for use with their own Spanish-speaking primary grade students, many of whom are taught by monolingual English-speaking teachers.

In other words, good decision-making on the part of policy-makers and practitioners is contingent on the quality of research available on the interventions and the knowledge and skills of these decision-makers regarding the values, characteristics, cultures, and learning needs of their populations. When there is not enough information about the intervention research, then decision-makers are handicapped in their ability to make predictions about the potential effectiveness of the intervention for their own populations and setting. They are also left with minimal guidance about the potential changes and modifications in the intervention that may be needed to assure success within their own cultural populations and settings.

According to Lincoln and Guba (1985), experts in the field of naturalistic and qualitative inquiry, transferability is one of four criteria for establishing the trustworthiness of qualitative findings. In brief, "transferability refers to the applicability of findings to other situations based on comparability with the research context" (Nastasi et al., 2004, p. 48). It is similar to the construct of external validity in traditional quantitative research methods, and is relevant to cultural considerations in EBI research. Assessments of transferability are enhanced with solid information about the cultural validity of the research process and findings.

Questions to Ask

There are many questions decision-makers should ask when considering use of an intervention for which evidence was documented in another setting or with a different population. Table 1 summarizes some of the main questions to consider. First, identify the similarities and differences between the people and context of those in the published EBI and the intended people and context where the intervention might be adopted. Second, if there are differences in the context, participants, and/or interventionists, carefully consider how to modify and adjust the EBI to match the targeted population and cultural context. Third, identify the mechanisms of change in the EBI and how these may be similar or different with the intended context and population. Fourth, consider using a participatory process by involving participants in all phases of the selection, adoption, and evaluation of the intervention. In other words, school psychologists need to be both culturally competent and skilled in the use of scientist-practitioner methods that allow for hypothesis testing, gathering and analyzing relevant data, and using the results to inform their practice. This is similar to the problem-solving approach used by a school psychologist who leads a team in the development of a positive behavior support plan. Upon seeing how the intervention is working, sometimes adjustments are needed in the behavior plan. The new data about the intervention process and outcomes are used to improve the precision and delivery of the intervention in a cyclical manner that leads to increased intervention efficacy. Fifth, evaluate how the intervention is working with the new targeted population, with particular attention to issues of internal, external, cultural, and ecological validity and the mechanisms of change as perceived by the participants.

TABLE 1. Questions to Ask When Considering Evidence About an Intervention and Possible Transportation and Adoption in a New Setting

1. What are the *similarities and differences* between the people and context of the study versus those of my work setting? Assess the transferability and generalizability.

   a. How do the community, setting, and environmental context compare with mine?

   b. How do the participants in the study compare with those in my setting? Do my intended participants hold similar beliefs, worldviews, and perspectives? (Include attention to salient cultural, economic, geographical, political, and psychological factors such as experiences of oppression, perceived power, and trust with interventionists, etc.)

   c. How do the interventionists compare with mine (e.g., similarity with target clients, level of training, perspectives and worldviews)?

2. When there are differences among the context, participants and/or interventionists, *what modifications* in the intervention or process of adopting the intervention would best take into account the cultures of my intended setting? Make adjustments to match the context and target population.

   a. Where can I get information to inform the design of the necessary modifications? (e.g., cultural brokers or guides, members of the cultural backgrounds prevalent in my target group, persons with different perspectives from my own)

   b. What assumptions am I making about the universality or cultural specificity of this intervention and my target setting, participants, interventionists, and cultural competence? How can I validate these assumptions?

   c. How will I know if these modifications are successful in adapting the intervention for use in my setting?

3. What is known about the *mechanisms of change* that make this intervention effective?

   a. In what ways might cultural diversity affect these mechanisms of change?

   b. Are these same mechanisms likely to occur in my intended setting and with the cultures of my population?

   c. How might these similarities and differences inform the adjustments I need to make in the intervention process?

4. How will I involve members of my target population (*participatory processes*) in the:

   a. Decision about whether to adopt and how to adapt this intervention for our setting?

   b. Collection of data on the process and outcomes of the intervention to determine how it is working and, if needed, where and what adjustments may be needed?

   c. Interpretation of process and outcome data?

5. What formative data will be used to *evaluate how the intervention is working* in the new setting and with the new groups of people?

   a. What hypotheses will help check the cultural, ecological, internal, and external validity of this transportation of the intervention to the new setting/context?

   b. What kind of data would be most informative about the mechanisms of change and how my target participants perceive the intervention, the process to evaluate it, and the interpretation of formative findings?

Further research and continued practice that is culturally informed are imperative. The available science is not yet current with the issues practitioners confront in work within a diverse world. At this point, we recommend that practitioners consider the following propositions as they proceed to make informed decisions about the interventions they use in their practice of school psychology:

1. Interventions that have not included diverse populations (among the intervention recipients, interventionists, and researchers) are yet unknown in terms of their effectiveness with other groups.
2. More intervention research with other, more diverse groups must be conducted, with designs that provide data regarding the transferability, generalization, and cultural validity of the intervention.
3. It is expected that adjustments may be needed for the intervention to be meaningful and successful for different cultural groups and/or in different contexts. Whether or not this will affect the outcome of the intervention is an empirical question that requires the collection and evaluation of data.

Naturalistic inquiry (e.g., Lincoln & Guba, 1985), with data collected in real settings of practice, is a valuable method of obtaining information that can inform the practice of school psychology in multicultural contexts. The participatory model (e.g., Nastasi et al., 2004), action research, qualitative research methods (see Nastasi & Schensul, 2005a, 2005b), and comparative case study approaches (e.g., Ingraham, 2003) are plausible ways to proceed in the absence of data. Once the revised version of the *Procedural and Coding Manual for Review of Evidence-Based Interventions* is complete, researchers can use this and the discussion in this paper to guide their research and more fully attend to culture throughout the EBI process. Practitioners can use the questions in Table 1 to guide their evaluation of existing EBIs and their decision-making regarding if and how to transport EBIs to their own setting of practice. Using naturalistic inquiry, with special attention to the proposed criteria, psychologists can systematically collect and evaluate their own data when using an intervention with a population that is different from that which was originally researched.

CONCLUSIONS AND RECOMMENDATIONS

Intervention recipients, interventionists, researchers, and the settings in which the interventions are delivered are all influenced by cultural considerations. The identification, selection, and implementation of EBIs for a culturally diverse world involve attending to the ways culture is represented in all phases of the research and intervention process. To date, the preponderance of research on interventions has been carried out primarily by researchers with interventionists and clients of primarily Caucasian, middle class backgrounds. When samples include participants of differing backgrounds, their numbers are often too small to be representative of the national population of students and families. Very little research has been conducted with sufficient numbers of ethnic minority or diverse populations (culturally, ethnically, racially, socio-economically) to inform intervention practice in today's diverse school and community settings. The importance of having an adequate research base to judge the effectiveness of these interventions by and with these populations is clear.

Thus, the critical question is whether interventions that have demonstrated success with non-representative samples can be expected to generalize to a diversity of clients and to those who may not share critical characteristics and fundamental stances, dispositions, and assumptions about the world. For example, is an intervention that has been shown to be effective with a predominately college town European American population likely to be effective with urban Latino, African American, Hispanic, and Asian American populations? Would adaptations that accommodate differences in these populations fundamentally alter the intervention? Does it matter if the person delivering the intervention is of the same cultural background as the clients? Until evidence is available to answer these questions, we recommend that practitioners proceed with caution when transporting interventions to new contexts. Practitioners will need to use both high levels of cultural competence and problem-solving skills in using an evidence-based process; they will need to collect and evaluate information to assure that interventions are appropriate and effective in the practitioner's context.

School psychologists have a fundamental role in bringing cultural competence and knowledge to their work with interventions. It is critical that they understand the multitude of ways that culture is expressed in EBIs and throughout their own intervention setting. The interventions they select, the process they use to deliver the interventions, the participants in the intervention process, and the interventionists themselves have significant influences on the intervention process and outcomes. Fully recognizing the ways culture can influence the intervention research, process, evaluation, and outcomes will enhance the potential for intervention effectiveness and success.

Culture pervades school psychology research, theory, and practice, and specifically the EBI approach, whether recognized or not. Both practitioners and researchers have a vital role in developing and using methods that more fully attend to cultural issues. In the effort to seek and use EBIs (i.e., interventions that have a scientific base to document their effectiveness), psychologists who are knowledgeable about the cultural issues prevalent throughout research and intervention processes will be best prepared to practice with competence in today's diverse world.

REFERENCES

American Psychological Association. (2003) Guidelines for multicultural education, training, research, practice, and organizational change for psychologists, *American Psychologist, 58* (5), 377-402.

Atkinson, D. R., Bui, U., & Mori, S. (2001). Multiculturally sensitive empirically treatments–An oxymoron? In J. G. Ponterotto, J. M. Casas, L. A. Suzuki, & C. M. Alexander (Eds.), *Handbook of multicultural counseling* (2nd ed., pp. 542-574). Thousand Oaks, CA: Sage.

Christenson, S. L., Carlson, C., & Valdez, C. R. (2002). Evidence-based interventions in school psychology: Opportunities, challenges, and cautions. *School Psychology Quarterly, 17* (4), 466-474.

Coleman, H. K. K., & Wampold, B. E. (2003). Challenges to the development of culturally relevant empirically supported treatment. In D. B. Pope-Davis, H.L.K. Coleman, W. Liu, & Toperek (Eds.), *Handbook of multicultural competencies* (pp. 227-246). Thousand Oaks, CA: Sage.

Gonzales, J. J., Ringelsen, H. L., & Chambers, D. A. (2002). The tangled and thorny path of science to practice: Tensions in interpreting and applying "evidence." *Clinical Psychology: Science and Practice, 9* (2), 204-209.

Hughes, J. N. (2000). The essential role of theory in the science of treating children: Beyond empirically supported treatments. *Journal of School Psychology, 38* (4), 301-330.

Ingraham, C. L. (2003). Multicultural consultee-centered consultation: When novice consultants explore cultural hypotheses with experienced teacher consultees. *Journal of Educational and Psychological Consultation, 14* (3 & 4), 329-362.

Ingraham, C. L., Oka, E. R., & Nastasi, B. (2004, August). *Developing cultural and methodological diversity in EBIs in school psychology.* Poster presented at the annual meeting of the American Psychological Association, Honolulu, Hawaii.

Ingraham, C. L., Oka, E. R., & Nastasi, B. (2005, January). *Infusing cultural validity criteria into the SP EBI scoring manual.* Poster presented at the National Multicultural Summit and Conference, Hollywood, CA.

Kratochwill, T. R., & Shernoff, E. S. (2003). Evidence-based practice: Promoting evidence-based intervention in school psychology. *School Psychology Quarterly, 18* (4), 389-408.

Kratochwill, T. R., & Stoiber, K. C. (2000). Empirically supported interventions and school psychology: Rationale and methodological issues–Part II. *School Psychology Quarterly, 15* (2), 233-253.

Kratochwill, T. R., & Stoiber, K. C. (2002a). Evidence-based interventions in school psychology: Conceptual foundations of the *Procedural and Coding Manual* of Division 16 and the Society for the Study of School Psychology Task Force. *School Psychology Quarterly, 17,* 341-389.

Kratochwill, T. R., & Stoiber, K. C. (Eds.) (2002b). *Procedural and coding manual for review of evidence-based interventions.* Authors. (EBI Manual 12/10/02)

Lincoln, Y. S., & Guba, E. G. (1985). *Naturalistic inquiry.* Beverly Hills: Sage.

Markus, H. R., & Kitayama, S. (1991). Culture and the self: Implications for cognition, emotion, and motivation, *Psychological Review, 98,* 224-253.

Nastasi, B. K., Moore, R. B., & Varjas, K. M. (2004). *School-based mental health services: Creating comprehensive and culturally specific programs.* Washington DC: American Psychological Association.

Nastasi, B. K., & Schensul, S. L. (2005a). Contributions of qualitative research to the validity of intervention research. *Journal of School Psychology, 43* (3), 177-195.

Nastasi, B. K., & Schensul, S. L. (Eds.) (2005b). Contributions of qualitative research to the validity of intervention research. Special issue of *Journal of School Psychology, 43* (3).

Ollendick, T. H. & King, N. J. (2004). Empirically supported treatments for children and adolescents: Advances toward evidence-based practice. In P. M. Barrett, & T. H. Ollendick (Eds.), *Handbook of interventions that work with children and adolescents: Prevention and treatment* (pp. 3-25). Hoboken, NJ: Wiley.

Peng, K., & Nisbett, R. E. (1999). Culture, dialectics, and reasoning about contradiction. *American Psychologist, 54* (9), 743-754.

Quintana, S. M., & Atkinson, D. R. (2002). A multicultural perspective on principles of empirically support interventions. *The Counseling Psychologist, 30* (2), 281-291.

Quintana, S. M., Troyano, N., & Taylor, G. (2001). Cultural validity and inherent challenges in quantitative methods for multicultural research. In J. G. Ponterotto, J. M. Casas, L. A. Suzuki, & C. M. Alexander (Eds.), *Handbook of multicultural counseling* (2nd ed., pp. 604-630). Thousand Oaks, CA: Sage.

Serlin, R. C., Wampold, B. E., & Levin, J. R. (2003). Should providers of treatment be regarded as a random factor?: If it ain't broke, don't 'fix' it. *Psychological Methods, 8,* 524-534.

Shweder, R., Goodnow, J., Hatano,G., LeVine, R. A., Markus, H., & Miller, P. (1998). The cultural psychology of development: One mind, many mentalities. In W. Damon (Series Ed.) and R. M. Lerner (Vol. Ed.), *Handbook of child psychology: Vol. I: Theoretical models of human development* (5th ed., pp. 865-937). New York: John Wiley.

Stoiber, K. C., & Kratochwill, T. R. (2000). Empirically supported interventions and school psychology: Rationale and methodological issues–Part I. *School Psychology Quarterly, 15* (1), 75-105.

Sue, S. (1998). In search of cultural competence in psychotherapy and counseling. *American Psychologist, 53*(4), 440-448.

Sue, S. (1999). Science, ethnicity, and bias: Where have we gone wrong? *American Psychologist, 54*(12), 1070-1077.

Thompson, V. L. S., Bazile, A., & Akbar, M. (2004). African Americans' perceptions of psychotherapy and psychotherapists. *Professional Psychology: Research and Practice, 35* (1), 19-26.

U.S. Department of Health and Human Services (2001). *Mental health: Culture, race, and ethnicity–A supplement to mental health: A Report of the Surgeon General.* Rockville, MD: U.S. Department of Health and Human Services, Substance Abuse and Mental Health Services Administration, Center for Mental Health Services.

Wampold, B. E. (2001). *The great psychotherapy debate: Models, methods, and findings.* Mahwah, NJ: Erlbaum.

Wampold, B. E. (2002). An examination of the bases of evidence-based interventions. *School Psychology Quarterly, 17* (4), 500-507.

doi:10.1300/J370v22n02_07

Multicultural Issues
in School Psychology Practice:
A Critical Analysis

Samuel O. Ortiz

St. John's University

SUMMARY. Once thought of largely as a sideline issue, multiculturalism is fast becoming a major topic on the central stage of psychology and practice. That cultural factors permeate the whole of psychological foundations and influence the manner in which the very scope of practice is shaped is undeniable. The rapidly changing face of the U.S. population will only ensure that more and more attention is paid to understanding the dynamic interplay between culture and behavior that forms the core of multiculturalism. Nowhere is this process more evident than in school psychology where another critical component, learning, is brought into the already complicated mix. In the articles contained in this special publication, the various authors attempt to illuminate this process by providing discussions and examples of the profound effect that culture has in the context of school-related psychological endeavors, such as consultation, counseling, and evaluation. They include theoretical considerations regarding evidence-based interventions (Ingraham & Oka, this volume) and assessment (Hitchcock, Sarkar, Nastasi, Burkholder, Varjas & Jayasena, this volume), as well as applied considerations that

---

Address correspondence to: Samuel O. Ortiz, Department of Psychology, St. John's University, 8000 Utopia Parkway, Jamaica, NY 11439.

[Haworth co-indexing entry note]: "Multicultural Issues in School Psychology Practice: A Critical Analysis." Ortiz, Samuel O. Co-published simultaneously in *Journal of Applied School Psychology* (The Haworth Press, Inc.) Vol. 22, No. 2, 2006, pp. 151-167; and: *Multicultural Issues in School Psychology* (ed: Bonnie K. Nastasi) The Haworth Press, Inc., 2006, pp. 151-167. Single or multiple copies of this article are available for a fee from The Haworth Document Delivery Service [1-800-HAWORTH, 9:00 a.m. - 5:00 p.m. (EST). E-mail address: docdelivery@haworthpress.com].

range from instructional consultation (Lopez, this volume), system/ community interventions (Hatzichristou, Lampropoulou & Lykitsakou, this volume), and bullying intervention (Varjas, Meyers, Henrich, Graybill, Dew, Marshall, Williams, Skoczylas & Avant, this volume), to home-school partnerships (Vazquez-Nuttall, Li & Kaplan, this volume). Clearly, the purpose of this special collection is to advance the somewhat limited research and knowledge-base related to multiculturalism. To that end, these articles are discussed critically with emphasis on both thematic elements that assist in illuminating the dynamics and processes that underlie multicultural school psychology and the various implications for the practice of school psychology with culturally diverse populations. doi:10.1300/J370v22n02_08 *[Article copies available for a fee from The Haworth Document Delivery Service: 1-800-HAWORTH. E-mail address: <docdelivery@haworthpress.com> Website: <http://www.HaworthPress.com> © 2006 by The Haworth Press, Inc. All rights reserved.]*

KEYWORDS. Cultural training, school psychology roles, environment and schools

Few factors affect the daily practice of school psychology more profoundly than those related to culture. The rapid changes in the ethnic diversity of the school-aged population in the United States suggests that issues related to culture will continue to become increasingly important and central to all aspects of practitioner's professional activities. Indeed, the very rationale and appeal of this special publication indicate a tremendous interest in the matter and a great need among school psychologists for information and assistance in developing and managing culturally competent practice.

The articles that comprise this publication are quite variable in focus yet they come together under a common umbrella known as multiculturalism. When applied to the practice of school psychology, the term takes on myriad forms as exemplified by the wide array of topics and activities addressed in this volume. The manifestation of multiculturalism in school psychology practice to be discussed herein consists of six applications that include evidence-based intervention (Ingraham & Oka, this volume), assessment (Hitchcock, Sarkar, Nastasi, Burkholder, Varjas & Jayasena, this volume), instructional consultation (Lopez, this volume), system/ community interventions (Hatzichristou, Lampropoulou & Lykitsakou, this volume), bullying intervention (Varjas, Meyers, Henrich, Graybill,

Dew, Marshall, Williams, Skoczylas & Avant, this volume), and home-school partnerships (Vazquez-Nuttall, Li & Kaplan, this volume). The articles represent a combination of both theoretical development and research-based findings that have significant implications not only for the practice of school psychology, but also for future research, training, and policy. The purpose of the present narrative is to critically examine the manner in which multiculturalism affects the practice of school psychology from the perspective of each particular application.

THEORETICAL CONSIDERATIONS

One of the more recent and prominent trends in school psychology as a whole is the movement toward the development and use of "evidence-based interventions" (EBI), sometimes referred to as "empirically supported treatments" (EST) (see Kratochwill & Shernoff, 2003; Ollendick & King, 2004; Stoiber & Kratochwill, 2000). It follows logically that intervention practices and procedures used in school psychology should have demonstrable scientific evidence that supports their use. More importantly, however, there also should be evidence regarding the population for whom a given intervention is effective and appropriate. This is the crux of the problem when multicultural issues are infused into the EBI discussion and forms the focus of the article by Ingraham and Oka (this volume).

Clearly, the issue of EBI and its relation to multiculturalism is critical because it affects the very generalizability of any intervention or treatment utilized in the practice of school psychology. When empirical studies provide support for a particular method, the degree of confidence that a practitioner can have regarding its applicability and efficacy with a multicultural population will depend heavily on the degree to which multicultural issues were part of the original design and validation. Given that the EBI movement is relatively new, there are very few studies that have directly addressed issues of multiculturalism or diversity apart from those included in this special issue. Thus, practitioners may well find themselves with a dilemma identified by Ingraham and Oka (this volume, p. 130):

Although there is a vast amount of intervention research, the process of reviewing, evaluating, and identifying interventions that meet the EBI criteria is still in the early stages. The result is that there are a limited number of interventions that have been identified as EBIs. . . . Practitioners can't wait until there is a substantial body of research with their intended populations and within their specific cultural context, yet our professional ethics advise that tools and interventions should be valid and reliable for the specific individuals with whom they are utilized. (APA, 2003)

Guidance toward the resolution of this dilemma is provided by Ingraham and Oka (this volume) and they rightly note that when multicultural issues are applied in the examination of EBIs that the issue boils down to one of generalizability. If a social-skills development program for 3rd grade students in a predominantly white, middle-class, suburban school district is found to be effective in the formation of better interpersonal skills, is it automatically applicable to other predominantly Hispanic 3rd graders from a low SES community in an urban setting? Maybe. Maybe not. Given the knowledge base in multicultural issues in psychology in general, it seems the latter position may be the correct one and at the very least practitioners need to exercise considerable caution in applying any treatment, even one considered to be an EBI. Unless and until EBIs emerge that have been validated in light of the various populations that might fall under the rubric of multicultural (i.e., African American, Hispanic, etc.), it will be difficult to know how applicable any such EBI may be for a given purpose and population.

The issue of generalizability, however, is much like a double-edged sword. On the one hand, it is fair to state that EBIs are effective primarily for the individuals on whom the intervention was validated and that its utility with populations that may be culturally different cannot be presumed. On the other hand, the very definition of EBI and its validation on a particular group means that it has been demonstrated to be absolutely valid for that group only. In a sense, from a broad perspective, every EBI demonstrates "cultural" validity in its own idiosyncratic way. That is, every population on whom an EBI is validated constitutes a unique "cultural" group, as defined by its own particular characteristics. Thus, an EBI is only so (i.e., evidence-based) and demonstrably efficacious for the very group, but not any other, on which the data were collected. Such a view of "culture" is of course, too restrictive, but illustrates the problems with defining particular groups on the basis of characteristics that may not lend themselves to precise definitions. Ingraham and Oka (this volume) note that the concept of cultural validity may need to be broadened in order to encompass meaningful groups and not artificially limit the applicability of research that may be informative, if not directly relevant for populations that may not have been the direct focus of the EBI.

One of the other major points discussed by Ingraham and Oka (this volume) revolves around the concept of external validity. Whereas issues of generalizability deal with whether a treatment or intervention may be applicable to one group or another, the issue of external validity deals with whether the constructs involved in the treatment or intervention retain the same properties and address or assess the very same intended constructs. For example, research on the measurement of cognitive abilities often focuses on demonstration of cross-cultural validity by showing that factor structures remain similar and that tests which cluster together for one population, do so with other populations (Carroll, 1993; Horn & Noll, 1997). Yet, it would be surprising if such relations did not hold across populations because validity, in this sense, is unlikely to be affected solely by a change in the population on whom such tests may be administered (Ortiz, 2002). What is more likely to change is whether the measured attribute is actually the same attribute the scale is purported to measure. With what degree of confidence can it be said that an EBI designed to reduce anger and increase anger management skills actually results in a reduction of anger and increase in anger management skills in elementary school Native American children? The fact that it can be shown that *measured* anger is reduced and *measured* anger management skills increased does not necessarily mean that it was these variables that changed. It may well have been others. Ingraham and Oka (this volume) cite researchers (e.g., Quintana, Troyana & Taylor, 2001) who have proposed that a new form of validity (cultural) be added to the existing types (i.e., internal, external, construct, etc.).

Consistent with this call for demonstrable cultural validity, in their article Hitchcock and colleagues (this volume) provide an excellent example regarding how cultural validity can be established for constructs of interest. They state:

> What complicates matters is that most psychological instruments do not adequately address the influence of culture on functioning, especially for ethnic minority groups (APA, 2003; Padilla, 2001; USDHHS, 1999, 2001). Some literature suggests that members of a cultural majority tend to be unaware of cultural influences (Sue, Bingham, Porche-Burke & Vasquez, 1999); not surprisingly, researchers often generate instruments with little regard for these

factors (Rogler, 1999). Failure to address cultural differences in assessment may therefore lead to problems with construct validity and subsequent efforts to develop interventions based on such assessment. (Hitchcock et al., this volume, p. 16)

By combining both qualitative (ethnographic) and quantitative approaches, Hitchcock and colleagues outline an extremely well thought out, mixed-method framework for identifying and validating psychological constructs. The focus of their efforts centered on self-concept among adolescents living in Sri Lanka. Rather than simply attempting to create a normative sample, Hitchcock and colleagues sought to gather a wide range of data with regard to the definition of key constructs and utilized focus groups to that end. This helped to ensure that not only were the definitions of concepts such as mental health/personal-social competence and adjustment culturally derived, but so too were the cultural mechanisms for socialization, identification of social stressors, mechanisms/personal resources for coping, and existing resources. This process not only uncovered culture-specific issues and information but eventually led to the identification of gender-based differences as well–differences that may not have come to light without the time taken to truly understand the population of interest.

It should be noted that it took two years of ethnographic research just to uncover enough culture-specific information with which to proceed to the development of appropriate instruments. Such patience and care in making sure the collected information reflects the nature of the construct of interest such that it can be appropriately operationalized. It is unlikely, however, that all researchers will demonstrate such diligence in the development of other scales or interventions and the attendant limitations of not doing so should be factored into the generalizability and validity of obtained results. The work by Hitchcock and colleagues emphasizes the need to engage in a deliberate and systematic process in order to develop culturally appropriate scales and assessment instruments. The typical practice of utilizing existing instruments developed in the U.S. for a mainstream population and then translating it into another language for use with individuals in other countries is not acceptable practice. Likewise, however, scales developed for populations outside the U.S. (e.g., Sri Lanka) are not automatically appropriate for individuals from that country living in the U.S. Not only do issues of acculturation begin to play a significant role in differentiating native residents of a country from immigrants from that country, but issues related to bilingualism also become particularly salient with respect to cultural validity, especially for school-aged children.

Ultimately, Ingraham and Oka (this volume) conclude that culture permeates the entire process of research and intervention. They provide three important recommendations for practitioners that can assist in their attempts to utilize EBIs. In general, they state (a) interventions that do not include diverse populations cannot be presumed to be effective with them; (b) much more research is needed before any intervention can demonstrate adequate generalizability and cultural validity; and (c) modifications or adaptations may be necessary when attempting to apply existing interventions to diverse populations, however, the effect of such changes and their impact will require additional research. The ability to follow these recommendations forms the basis of some of the skills that reflect a broader component of professional expertise called cultural competence and is a theme that occurs throughout all the articles contained herein.

APPLIED CONSIDERATIONS

Of the four articles in this collection that dealt with the infusion of multicultural issues in an applied manner, three of them focused primarily on the application of multicultural issues in specific areas of practice. Lopez (this volume) discusses the various aspects of instructional consultation with teachers of English language learners (ELLs) in the U.S. Hatzichristou and colleagues (this volume) address cultural factors in the development of system/community interventions with school children in Greece. Varjas and colleagues (this volume) describe a bullying intervention project in an urban, multiethnic school system. And Vazquez-Nuttall, Li, and Kaplan (this volume) discuss a case study involving the development of better home-school partnerships with culturally diverse families.

In demonstrating the application of multicultural issues in practice, two of the articles (Hatzichristou et al., this volume; Varjas et al., this volume) either discuss or utilize frameworks adapted from Nastasi, Moore and Varjas (2004) known as the Participatory Culture Specific Consultation Model (PCSCM) and the Participatory Culture Specific Intervention Model (PCSIM), and will be referred generically here as the Participatory Culture Specific Model (PCSM; Nastasi et al., 2004). The main components of these models include ethnographic research methods, an action research and participatory consultation processes, and cultural specificity, albeit the entire model is represented by as many as 11 distinct phases (Nastasi et al., 2004). An example of the application of this framework with respect to scale development and construct fidelity was evident in the work of Hitchcock and colleagues (this volume) discussed previously. In the current research, however, the focus is on application of the model in the delivery of intervention and consultation services.

These articles (Hatzichristou et al., this volume; Varjas et al., this volume) demonstrate both the utility and flexibility of the PCSM with respect to intervention. The latter was targeted at the individual level and was designed to address issues of bullying in a multiethnic urban school. The project sought to directly influence the climate associated with bullying in one school system using the various component phases of the PCSM, as applied at the research level (Phases 1 through 6) and subsequent intervention program (Phases 7 through 11). According to the authors, the students of the middle school where the project took place reported that bullying was related to ethnicity, socioeconomic status (i.e., class), and perceived sexual orientation (Varjas et al., this volume). They also reported that the school was ethnically diverse being about evenly split between African American and Caucasian students, with small percentages of Asian American, Hispanic and multiracial individuals. According to the students involved in the project, their major concerns regarding bullying revolved around issues of race, physical differences, and lack of adult response to bullying complaints.

With respect to the issue of multiculturalism, however, it is not clear whether the bullying project actually incorporated the concept. Certainly, the term "culture" is quite broad and should be used in an inclusive manner whenever possible. The attention to the issues raised by the students does indicate a focus on at least one typical cultural variable, race. But the response of the students indicate problems related to either fitting in or not fitting in within their own racial groups, not difficulties between ethnic groups or more precisely, between cultures. In addition, because the project utilized existing measures of internalizing problems, school problems, and personal adjustment, it begs the question as to why no attempt was made to validate the constructs for the cultures involved. If the measures (developed for the mainstream U.S. population) were already appropriate for the groups involved, then where is the actual multicultural focus in the intervention?

In defense of the authors of the project, the behavioral evidence of bullying was clearly present and the nature of it was accurately identified. However, in the application of a multicultural perspective, the authors may have missed an opportunity to better exemplify multicultural issues. For example, the student responses regarding not fitting in, physical differences, and lack of adult support might have been conceptualized as issues related to the culture of skin color, culture of obesity, and culture of power. Indeed, the three themes that emerged from the group interviews and discussions were cited as perceived sexual orientation, poor hygiene, and being new to the school. Again, these may have been better served and understood by translating them into a cultural framework, namely various forms of the culture of prejudice and intolerance. Doing so is necessary in order to reveal the cultural dynamics that are crucial to the eventual success and effectiveness of interventions.

As noted previously, there is as much danger in defining culture too broadly as there is in defining it too restrictively. What is clear, however, is that the development and application of interventions in a diverse setting or with a multiethnic population does not automatically make it an example of multicultural practice. The issues that emerge as the focus in such situations might well be the very same as would come out of research with any group. School psychology practices are imbued with a multicultural focus only when the dynamics of cultural clashes are identified and made the focus of a particular intervention or activity. Multicultural competence for practitioners lies not so much in understanding every unique or idiosyncratic characteristic of different cultural groups but more in the ability to recognize when and where cultural issues might be operating in any aspect of practice (Fletcher-Janzen & Ortiz, in press; Ortiz, 2006; Ortiz & Flanagan, 2002).

Hatzichristou and colleagues (this volume) also describe an intervention project in their article, although it is targeted at the systems/community rather than individual level. The importance of understanding and recognizing the cultural dynamics that may operate in the attempt to develop and provide interventions is perhaps even more critical at the systems level. The authors state:

> Since a *system* is considered to be something more dynamic than the total of its components, it might be useful to adopt a '*metacultural perspective*' that considers the multicultural systems as integrating the various elements of its consisting cultural groups into new dynamic outcomes. (emphasis in original; Hatzichristou et al., this volume, p. 110)

Toward the goal of a metacultural perspective, Hatzichristou and colleagues (this volume) make it a point to distinguish between the terms "multicultural" and "cross-cultural." The former term implies the simple existence of many cultures within a setting and the recognition of qualities that distinguish them. As such, multicultural equates to a pluralistic society or one that has many ethnicities within it (i.e., polyethnic). In contrast, cross-cultural describes the diversity among and the process of interaction between groups across different settings. It is perhaps subtle, but the language is one of inclusion and concentrates on recognizing the dynamic interplay between the cultures of interest. Even some of the titles of the articles in this volume use the term multicultural (e.g., Ingraham & Oka, this volume) whereas others use the term cross-cultural (e.g., Hitchcock et al., this volume).

Hatzichristou and colleagues (this volume) sought to implement a primary prevention program aimed at enhancing social and emotional learning in children in public schools in Greece. Although they acknowledge the PCSM framework, they developed their own integrative framework that synthesized various conceptual domains in school psychology, including the scientist-practitioner model, a systemic approach to assessment and intervention, the role and function of practitioners, and a systemic approach to professional development. This framework served as an alternative model of school psychology practice and was instituted in four phases. In Phase I, the authors gathered empirical data to establish a profile of an "average" Greek student relative to areas of competence, prevalence of psychosocial problems, relations between psychosocial adjustment and academic performance, and the effect of family status and city size on functioning. Phase II focused on the individual level (identification of at-risk students with unmet needs), whereas Phase III expanded into a school and community-based needs assessment. Phase IV involved implementation of the primary prevention program aimed at enhancing the mental health needs of Greek students. Overall, the project demonstrates that it is not only possible, but desirable, to link current theory and research with practice, adjust to the culture-specific needs of individuals, and incorporate multidimensional assessments within the context of multicultural school psychology service delivery.

The third article in this applied group deals with instructional consultation with teachers that focuses on the needs of English language learners (ELLs). This demonstration is slightly different than those discussed previously in that it deals with consultation, as opposed to intervention, but also because the cultural issues in this case go beyond differences in ethnicity and include problems associated with the dual-language nature of ELLs, and more importantly, the manner in which they are provided instruction. That is, the target population in this case is not simply culturally different, but different by virtue of the fact that they represent individuals who are on various trajectories related to becoming circumstantial bilinguals (i.e., by force of circumstance rather than by choice). Instructional consultation in this context becomes rather salient in the respect that student achievement and academic progress is tied directly to the type of instruction provided (Ramirez, Yuen, Ramey & Pasta, 1991; Thomas & Collier, 1997, 2002), irrespective of other relevant cultural issues, such as level of acculturation. Lopez makes this point clear:

> The shift in this approach comes from examining the ELL student, not in isolation and as a "deficient" learner, but as a learner who is demonstrating expected developmental transitions within the second language acquisition process, or as a learner who may be demonstrating difficulties because of problems inherent to the instructional system (e.g., a poor match between the instructional components and the students' knowledge and/or skills). (Lopez, this volume, p. 63)

Training and education in second language acquisition and instructional pedagogy for ELLs is not common in school psychology. Accordingly, Lopez (this volume) outlines the key questions practitioners should explore with consultees regarding the development of their ELL students. These include how the student is functioning in English within the contexts of social and academic language skills, what student variables are affecting the second language acquisition process, and within what stage of second language acquisition is the student functioning. In addition, when the instructional consultation process moves to a focus on tasks, or what is to be learned, Lopez provides a list of questions that can assist practitioners in determining whether the instruction is sufficiently comprehensible (a major factor in the development of linguistic and academic competence). The degree to which there is a match or mismatch between a student's instructional needs and the instruction provided is at the heart of the consultation process. Given the many and varied factors related to the instruction of ELLs, the potential for such conflicts is increased significantly.

Once the focus of the consultation process shifts to treatment, unfortunately its limitations become evident in that resolution of instructional issues with ELLs may not be attainable within the context of classroom instruction. It is likely that very few districts would be willing to completely re-structure their curricula for ELLs were it pointed out that it would improve achievement for all ELLs. Given the fact that the most common program (traditional, pull-out ESL services) used across the U.S. leads to the worst academic outcomes (Crawford, 1999; Cummins, 2000; Thomas & Collier, 1997, 2002), practitioners will find no shortage of work helping teachers do what they can under conditions that are clearly less than optimal. Such is the nature of how cultural issues affect school psychology practice. Political, social, and even economic issues above and beyond the classroom environment or learning needs of the individual are likely to influence the condition and manner of psychological service delivery. In cases such as that illustrated in Lopez (this volume), the often controversial nature of some multicultural issues (i.e., bilingual education) may well create difficulties in the process that would not otherwise exist when dealing with mainstream populations and topics.

The final article dealing with applied considerations examined issues related to the creation and development of home-school partnerships with culturally diverse families (Vazquez-Nuttall et al., this volume). In this sense it is neither a typical intervention nor a strict form of consultation but rather combines elements of both. The advantages and outcomes related to improved home-school partnerships (including parent-school and parent-home relationships) are well known and discussed by Vazquez-Nuttall and colleagues. They then offer some valuable insight into the problems that arise when multicultural issues are entered into the equation. In recognition of the research that indicates that traditional family involvement practices appear to have limited effectiveness with culturally diverse families, four main reasons are offered for such apparent failure, including the fact that the very idea of parental involvement is based on values that belong primarily to the mainstream, middle-class, two-parent family with traditional values who have long resided in the U.S. The other reasons involve the limited and variable quality of information and guidance provided parents to help their children, lack of recognition that parents from diverse backgrounds may not know or understand their roles in such partnerships, a failure to understand the importance of extended relatives in the family structure, and the tendency to view cultural groups as more homogenous than they actually are.

In response to the call for use of EBIs, Vazquez-Nuttall and colleagues (this volume) describe several existing parent involvement programs–only some of which were developed specifically for use with diverse families. However, it is unclear as to whether any of the programs were subjected to the type of standards described previously regarding generalizability and construct validity. Nonetheless, such programs represent the type of research that will no doubt lead to programs that will be effective and appropriate in their multicultural focus.

CONCLUSION

The six articles that comprise this special collection all provide examples regarding the nature of multiculturalism and its application in school psychology service delivery. Some articles addressed theoretical or research-oriented issues (Ingraham & Oka, this volume; Hitchcock et al., this volume) whereas others focused on more applied issues (Hatzichristou et al., this volume; Lopez, this volume; Varjas et al., this volume; Vazquez-Nuttall et al., this volume). Despite the differences in focus or process, there are some common themes that run throughout the articles and which serve as a basic foundation upon which school psychologists might seek to develop multicultural competence in their own practices.

One of the central issues identified across the articles is the need to implement those interventions that are empirically supported. Several authors noted, however, that there is almost no research regarding the effectiveness of a particular program for use with individuals from cultural or linguistic backgrounds different from those on whom the interventions were validated. In addition, although EBIs and ESTs are not evaluative procedures per se, they may well remain subject to the same standards and requirements that guide all practices and procedures utilized with diverse populations. For example, both IDEA 2004 and the *Standards for Educational and Psychological Tests* (AERA, APA & NCME, 1999) require that any method or procedure not be discriminatory on a racial or cultural basis. In addition, other provisions stipulate that the procedures be provided in a student's native language or other mode of communication, that procedures be validated for the purpose intended in their use, and that no single procedure be relied upon solely in making educational decisions. Vazquez-Nuttall and colleagues (this volume) provided specific examples of programs that were designed specifically for particular cultural groups. However, few EBIs or ESTs, including those noted in their article, have been fully evaluated in light of these standards and with regard to their efficacy with students from diverse cultural and linguistic backgrounds and there is precious little research available to determine whether such interventions remain valid and equitable for use with students from diverse backgrounds. Until such time, practitioners must use their best judgment to determine the degree to which any EBI will or will not be appropriate for a given population or application in a culturally diverse setting.

A second theme that emerged from the articles relevant to school psychology practice and competency development involved issues related to the nature and definition of culture itself. Culture can be defined broadly or narrowly. It can be inclusive or exclusive. It can highlight differences among groups or it can emphasize commonalities between them. Too often, culture is defined in terms of ethnicity, race, or even country of origin. And although such conceptions of culture have merit in some instances, none of them should be viewed as an acceptable substitute or proxy. It seems that culture refers primarily to a group of individuals who on the basis of one or more particular characteristics share a similar experience that engenders similar world views, attitudes, beliefs, behaviors, and norms. Note that the characteristics need not be based on skin color or race. Children with disabilities (e.g., deaf or blind) share an overarching personal characteristic that virtually assures they will have a similar cultural experience.

The third major and final theme that permeated the articles discussed in this narrative revolved around the essence of cultural competence itself. It was noted that cultural competence cannot be defined simply as knowledge of the particular characteristics of a given cultural group. Such information is important but does not automatically imbue practitioners with the necessary skills with which to effectively and appropriately serve multicultural populations or implement culturally appropriate interventions or treatments. Hatzichristou and colleagues (this volume) provided an eloquent statement of the fundamental aspect of cultural competence:

> In terms of multicultural community interventions, the development of cultural awareness and understanding that requires acknowledgement of similarities and differences between one's own culture and other cultures is an important prerequisite for effective system intervention within a multicultural context. (p. 109)

The premise here is that practitioners need not have or develop an entirely new repertoire of culture-specific skills or knowledge in order to apply EBIs effectively through intervention, consultation, or other types of services to diverse populations or in multicultural settings. A better goal for practitioners seems to be development of the ability to recognize when cultural factors, or differences in culture, are operating and affecting treatment and intervention attempts (Ortiz, 2006). The ability to do so will serve practitioners well and enhance their work with a wide variety of children and families with whom they may lack specific knowledge regarding culture-specific backgrounds and information.

Ultimately, success in the application of multicultural issues in school psychology service delivery will depend largely on the degree to which practitioners demonstrate a clear sense of respect for the individuals they seek to serve. According to Ortiz and Flanagan (2002):

> Intervening effectively with students and families will come more from a genuine respect of their native values, beliefs, and attitudes than anything else that might be said or done, especially when their views run counter to beliefs that may be held so dearly. In such cases it must be remembered that school psychologists are not often in positions where they are designing interventions for themselves. Rather, the intervention is for others and they will only be successful in so far as they are culturally relevant to the children and families for whom they are intended. (p. 353)

As practitioners await the execution of appropriate cross-cultural research and the buildup of demonstrated EBIs, they will need to acknowledge the limitations regarding what they may be able to do validly at the present time. Maintaining respect for their target populations may determine the eventual success of any type of service delivery, empirically supported or otherwise. Any attempt on the part of practitioners to understand and appreciate the world views of the children and family they seek to serve cannot help but promote better cross-cultural relations and build more effective working alliances.

REFERENCES

American Educational Research Association, American Psychological Association, & National Council on Measurement in Education (1999). *Standards for educational and psychological testing (3rd ed.)* Washington, DC: American Educational Research Association.

American Psychological Association (2003). Guidelines on multicultural education, training, research, practice, and organizational change for psychologists. *American Psychologist, 58,* 377-402.

Carroll, J.B. (1993). *Human cognitive abilities: A survey of factor-analytic studies.* New York: Cambridge University Press.

Crawford, J. (1999). *Bilingual education: History, politics, theory, and practice* (4th revised edition). Los Angeles, CA: Bilingual Education Services, Inc.

Cummins, J. (2000). *Language, power and pedagogy: Bilingual children in the crossfire.* Clevedon, England: Multilingual Matters.

Fletcher-Janzen, E. & Ortiz, S. O. (in press). Cultural competence in the use of IQ tests with culturally and linguistically diverse children. *Journal of School Psychology.*

Hatzichristou, C., Lampropoulou, A. & Lykitsakou, K. (2006). Addressing cultural factors in development of system interventions. *Journal of Applied School Psychology, 22* (2), 103-126.

Hitchcock, J.H., Sarkar, S., Nastasi, B.K., Burkholder, G., Varjas, K. & Jayasena, A. (2006). Validating culture- and gender-specific constructs: A mixed-method approach to advance assessment procedures in cross-cultural settings. *Journal of Applied School Psychology, 22* (2), 13-33.

Horn, J. L., & Noll, J. (1997). Human cognitive capabilities: Gf-Gc theory. In D. P. Flanagan, J. L. Genshaft, & P. L. Harrison (Eds.), *Contemporary intellectual assessment: Theories, tests, and issues* (pp. 53-91). New York: Guilford.

Ingraham, C.L., & Oka, E. R. (2006). Multicultural issues in evidence-based interventions. *Journal of Applied School Psychology, 22* (2), 127-149.

Kratochwill, T. R., & Shernoff, E. S. (2003). Evidence-based practice: Promoting evidence-based intervention in school psychology. *School Psychology Quarterly, 18* (4), 389-408.

Lopez, E. C. (2006). Targeting English Language Learners, tasks, and treatments in instructional consultation. *Journal of Applied School Psychology, 22* (2), 59-79.

Nastasi, B., Moore, R. B., & Varjas, K. M. (2004). *School-based mental health services: Creating comprehensive and culturally specific programs.* Washington, DC: American Psychological Association.

Ollendick, T. H. & King, N. J. (2004). Empirically supported treatments for children and adolescents: Advances toward evidence-based practice. In P. M. Barrett, & T. H. Ollendick (Eds.), *Handbook of interventions that work with children and adolescents: Prevention and treatment* (pp. 3-25). Hoboken, NJ: Wiley.

Ortiz, S. O. (2006). Multicultural Issues in Working with Children and Families: Responsive intervention in the educational setting. In Menutti, R.B., Freeman, A. & Christner, R.W. (Eds.) *Cognitive Behavioral Interventions in Educational Settings: A handbook for practice* (pp. 21-36). New York: Brunner-Routledge Publishing.

Ortiz, S. O. (2002). Best Practices in Nondiscriminatory Assessment. In A. Thomas & J. Grimes (Eds.) *Best Practices in School Psychology IV* (pp. 1321-1336). Washington, DC: National Association of School Psychologists.

Ortiz, S. O. & Flanagan, D. P. (2002). Best Practices in Working with Culturally Diverse Children and Families. In A. Thomas & J. Grimes (Eds.) *Best Practices in School Psychology IV* (pp. 337-351). Washington, DC: National Association of School Psychologists.

Quintana, S. M., Troyano, N., & Taylor, G. (2001). Cultural validity and inherent challenges in quantitative methods for multicultural research. In J. G. Ponterotto, J. M.

Casas, L. A. Suzuki, & C. M. Alexander (Eds.), *Handbook of multicultural counseling* (2nd ed., pp. 604-630). Thousand Oaks, CA: Sage.

Ramirez, J. D., Yuen, S.D., Ramey, D.R. & Pasta, D.J. (1991). *Final Report: Longitudinal study of structured English immersion strategy, early-exit and late-exit transitional bilingual education programs for language-minority children (Vols. I and II).* San Mateo, CA: Aguirre International.

Rogler, L.H. (1999). Methodological sources of cultural insensitivity in mental health research. *American Psychologist, 54,* 424-433.

Stoiber, K. C., & Kratochwill, T. R. (2000). Empirically supported interventions and school psychology: Rationale and methodological issues–Part I. *School Psychology Quarterly, 15* (1), 75-105.

Sue, D. W., Bingham, R. P., Porche-Burke, L., & Vasquez, M. (1999). The diversification of psychology: A multicultural revolution. *American Psychologist, 54,* 1061-1069.

Thomas, W. P. & Collier, V. P. (1997, December). *School effectiveness for language minority students.* Washington, DC: National Clearinghouse for Bilingual Education. Available online at: http://www.ncbe.gwu.edu/ncbepubs/resource/effectiveness/index.htm

Thomas, W.P., & Collier, V.P. (2002). A *national study of school effectiveness for language minority students' long-term academic achievement (Final Paper No. 1.1).* Santa Cruz, CA: University of California, Center for Research on Education, Diversity & Excellence.

U.S. Department of Health and Human Services (1999). *Mental health: A report of the Surgeon General.* Rockville, MD: U.S. Department of Health and Human Services, Substance Abuse and Mental Health Administration, Center for Mental Health Services, National Institutes of Health, National Institute of Mental Health.

U.S. Department of Health and Human Services (2001). *Mental health: Culture, race, and ethnicity–A supplement to mental health: A report of the Surgeon General.* Rockville, MD: U.S. Department of Health and Human Services, Substance Abuse and Mental Health Administration, Center for Mental Health Services.

Varjas, K., Meyers, J., Henrich, C.C., Graybill, E.C., Dew, B.J., Marshall, M.L., Williams, Z., Skoczylas, R.B. & Avant, M. (2006). Using a participatory culture-specific intervention model to develop a peer victimization model. *Journal of Applied School Psychology, 22* (2), 35-57.

Vazquez-Nuttall, E., Li, C., & Kaplan, J.P. (2006). Home-school partnerships with culturally diverse families: Challenges and solutions for school personnel. *Journal of Applied School Psychology, 22* (2), 81-102.

doi:10.1300/J370v22n02_08

Index